The
Great Assassins

The
Great Assassins

JUDGE
GERALD SPARROW

ARCO PUBLISHING COMPANY, INC.
New York

Published by ARCO PUBLISHING COMPANY, Inc.
219 Park Avenue South, New York, N.Y. 10003

Library of Congress Catalog Card Number 69-16270

Arco Book Number 668-01897-6

Printed in Great Britain

*This book has been set in Times,
on Antique Wove paper by Anchor Press, and
bound by Wm. Brendon, both of Tiptree Essex*

Contents

I

Author to Reader

WHEN my publishers suggested to me that great assassinations might make a fruitful and intriguing subject for a book, I liked the idea. I suppose it was the fact that for many years I had been a lawyer that made me, as a first step, find out exactly what an assassin was and in what assassination consisted.

I have always found words wonderful, for they are the battered survivors of so much history. Occasionally, of course, they assume meanings which they were never meant to assume. For instance, the word 'alibi', which in England still means the ability to prove that you were not in a certain place at a certain time but in another place, in the United States has degenerated into meaning no more than an excuse. Likewise the word 'problem', which originally indicated a situation or a mathematical puzzle capable of exact solution, has now been so broadened that it includes almost anything—'problem children', 'problem wives' and 'problem husbands'.

The word 'assassin' is one of those which has stormed through the pages of history from the East and come out still bearing the pungent flavour of its original meaning. Obviously the assassin is a treacherous killer or one who undertakes to kill treacherously. In the latter interpretation we have the suggestion that there are men lurking in the wings manipulating the fanatical puppet. In the time of the Crusades the 'Old Man of the Mountains' sent his henchmen to murder the Christians. Today we derive the word from the medieval French who, of course, received it from the Latin *assassinus*.

This is interesting enough but if we probe a little further then the real fanaticism which lurks around the assassin reaches out to us, for the word is derived from the Arabic *hashshash* and the word *hashishiyy* which indicated that the man being described was an eater of hashish.

Now hashish is not one of your deadly addictive drugs like opium, and the opium derivatives, but it is a powerful drug and, under its spell, the hashish eater, or even the hashish smoker, loses his sense of fear and also to a great extent his power to reason. If one idea has been implanted in his mind he will pursue that idea with absolute dedication until the desired result is achieved. All the questions he might ask himself—Have I any right to do this thing? Can I succeed in my mission? If I do succeed what is going to happen to me?—never occur to him. The effect of taking the drug in large quantities is to blot out all other considerations from his mind. He has, in fact, become a fanatical killer, usually with one victim in view, and it is because of this remorseless attitude and blind determination regardless of consequences that he so often succeeds where rational men might fail.

The smoking of hashish in moderation is quite common in North Africa and is indulged in not only by the local people but by some of the European residents. When they return to Europe as a rule they do not have too much difficulty in giving up the habit, but even taken in this way hashish has peculiar effects largely on the optic nerve and eyesight. It is very unwise to take hashish before driving a car, as the road may appear to be much larger than it really is, an assumption likely to lead to chaos.

Although assassination goes back to the Arab fanatic whose absolute faith in the Prophet and whose belief in Paradise formed a basis on which the drugs of the East could act to make a dedicated killer, assassination in more modern times has often been political rather than religious and the men who have prepared or perpetrated these murders—for that is what they are—are usually moved not by any stimulation of drugs but by ambition, revenge, or dedication to a philosophy.

In this book I am going to deal mainly with such modern assassinations. For instance, Trotsky, safe it was thought in his charming Mexican home five thousand miles away from his arch-enemy Stalin, was hunted down and murdered to satisfy Stalin's insatiable appetite for revenge and to abate his fear that as long as Trotsky lived the revolution had an able and greatly respected alternative leader.

The assassination of President Kennedy seems to have been a more carefully laid plot than at first we were led to suppose. The fact that the murderer, while still in police custody, was promptly murdered himself, thus silencing him for ever, was no accident. Moreover there is a great deal of evidence, both direct and circumstantial, that goes to show that there were other killers who fired at the presidential motorcade on the fatal day. It is at least possible that, as the findings of the Warren Commission are forgotten, we shall be faced with a political plot of sinister and dreadful implications. There is some ground for thinking that the dead President's widow believes that the truth has not yet been told. Certain it is that the killers of President Kennedy, on whom rested so much liberal and progressive hope in America and throughout the world, were cold and calculating men in the modern tradition of political murder.

The killing of Count Bernadotte by the Jewish Stern Gang again was a deliberate murder by political thugs who had a long record of evil and who, as a matter of policy, were ruthless killers of anyone whom they believed stood in their way. The killing of Sir Henry Wilson in London on June 22nd, 1922, was likewise a cold and deliberate murder by Irish Nationalists. All these crimes, political in their motivation, contained no element of hot, drugged fanaticism. They were planned with the utmost care, executed with dreadful precision.

Perhaps we have to go to the East to recapture the old authentic flavour of assassination, a mixture of misguided religious fervour and mad belief in the efficacy of murder. Mahatma Gandhi, loved by the people of India, and regarded by many as a Christ-like figure, was killed by a youth who believed he had to commit this terrible deed. To this day it has not been established, beyond all doubt, who implanted the idea in his mind.

King Abdullah of Jordan was assassinated in somewhat the same way as he left a mosque in Jerusalem with his entourage, including the present King Hussein of Jordan. King Hussein described to me what happened when I was in Amman and I have taken his description as the text of this assassination in this book.

Occasionally it is interesting to hurry back through the years and to speculate on the oldest and greatest assassinations of all time. For instance, was Julius Caesar really assassinated because he threatened to become an arbitrary dictator? There is remarkably little evidence of this. He seems to have regarded himself as the voice of the empire much in the same way as President de Gaulle regards himself as the spirit of France. Occasionally, like the French President, he would speak of himself in the third person. But this is not necessarily a sign of a megalomaniac. It may even be an indication that the person concerned still distinguishes between his public manifestation and his private individuality. The use of the royal 'We' in Britain until recently arose out of the same thinking. For instance, King George V distinguished very clearly between the Emperor of India and the Squire of Sandringham. It is at least possible that Shakespeare, who was a storyteller of genius and always refused to be unduly inhibited by historical fact, has misled us all. It may be that Caesar was killed because ambitious men were tempted by the prospect of manipulating world power.

Assassination never seems to die out. The 'disappearance' of Ben Barka, the liberal Moroccan leader, while on a visit to France is almost certainly a very modern example of murder to order. With the growth of espionage, too, we shall probably see an increase in political killing, for when Fleming wrote of his hero James Bond being 'licensed to kill' he did not exaggerate. In the epic struggle between the East and the West to learn each other's atomic secrets the life of a man means nothing to those engaged in this deadly business. So perhaps assassination, so far from decreasing, will actually multiply in the years immediately ahead of us.

I have considered very carefully whether to include in this book certain 'judicial killings', such as the execution of Charles I and the execution of Eichmann, the Nazi monster, kidnapped by Israeli agents while residing in South America. It is quite possible that in the future we shall regard the war-crime trials that followed the second great war as trials that came within this category. The hallmark, of course, of such killings is that the crime is invented after the deed has been done and not before.

Because for many years I was resident in the East I have included in this book some Eastern assassinations. They have a flavour entirely their own. For instance, King Thibaw, the last king of Burma, had quite a number of his potential rivals assassinated. In one particular palace purge no less than twenty-two men who had been unfortunate enough to incur the royal displeasure were disposed of and buried some miles from the palace. In order to make sure that the bodies would not rise up in protest a team of elephants was used to tread the ground hard until indeed there was no possibility of life remaining. It might be thought that the death of these unfortunate men would have been made certain much earlier but some of them were princes of Ava and traditional Burmese custom, which King Thibaw observed with punctilious respect, laid it down that the body of a prince could not be touched by his executioners. He was therefore placed in a golden sack and beaten to death without the executioners having contact with his person. Of course, as they could not see him they could not be quite certain that he was really dead or had merely been battered into unconsciousness. Hence the elephants applying their enormous weight to the burial ground.

A long correspondence took place between the King's ministers and the British authorities in Lower Burma who were protesting against these arbitrary killings and all the letters from the Burmese side were headed 'disposal and putting aside business'. This delightful euphemism is not uncharacteristic of the attitude of Eastern rulers who feel themselves impelled to take forceful measures against their enemies. In the same category would come the killings by the Empress of China of her lovers. It never seems to have occurred to her that these acts were anything except wise and inevitable disposals in the state interest.

In my own experience of Eastern assassination, centred very largely on Siam, I have noted that in the Orient assassination has a very individual flavour so I have included two stories of Siamese assassinations in this book. Usually one reads about assassinations in the newspapers. They are a seven days' wonder. Occasionally, as in the case of President Kennedy, they refuse to die and the public become uncomfortably aware that many facts have been concealed from them, facts that might incriminate public figures and reveal a hidden plot. But on one occasion I was actually present at an assassination, or present so soon after the shot had been fired that I was able to witness the sudden unrehearsed chaos that follows when a deeply venerated figure is struck down. In this case the murdered man was very young. He was King Ananda of Siam and he was shot on the 9th June 1946 in the King's bedchamber in the Barompinam Palace in Bangkok. Because of my nearness to this terrible assassination I have made it the first story in this book.

There is one odd thing concerning assassination. The actual killer is almost invariably caught and killed himself, except in cases of espionage murder, where great care is taken to get the agent responsible for the act clear of

danger in time. This is often possible because the victim
is usually killed privately. But in the case of political
assassinations these by their nature are usually very public, often taking place on great occasions when the killer
has no chance of escape. One would imagine, therefore,
that assassins would be very hard to find, but apparently
they are not. Quite recently the Prime Minister of
South Africa was assassinated quite openly in the Parliamentary Building in Cape Town. The man had no
hope whatever of escaping from the scene of his horrible
crime. This makes one think that in all assassinations
it is essential to probe far beyond the killer to find out, if
possible, who it was who planned and plotted the crime
and left someone else to execute it and suffer the penalty.

I hope it is clear from this outline of assassination that
we are dealing with a complex and intriguing branch of
murder. In fact it is typical that in assassination the word
'murder' is hardly ever used. Even the newspapers will
usually report the matter not as murder as such but as
assassination which, in some way, is regarded in a somewhat different light. There is no reason why we should
adopt any double vision about this matter. For us assassins
are murderers and the fact that their crime may be inspired by what they regard as good political motives
makes it murder no less. I suppose that a case could be
made out to justify the assassination of a tyrant. For instance, the assassination of Mussolini by Italian partisans,
revolting though it was, might be excused on these
grounds, but after a rather long experience of murderers of
all varieties in many countries I am inclined to dislike
them as a race and to regard political motivation as a very
poor excuse.

However, we must confess that the assassin, from the
point of view of literature, is in a class by himself. Often
the men who arrange assassinations are playing for the
very highest stakes. Sometimes the result of their action
may be momentous and lead to great change or great
calamity as was the case in the founding of the Soviet

Union or in the genesis of the first world war. For this reason assassinations tend to be more dramatic and perhaps more worthy of study than domestic murder. They are often the outcome of political passion. They are conceived sometimes in hatred, sometimes in idealism. They often disrupt a scene of great grandeur and rejoicing. The shot rings out, the dagger is thrust, an idol is bleeding and dying. This is drama at its highest, but we must also try in this book to probe the mind of the assassin. Is he, almost invariably, a subject for the psychiatrist? Or is he just a cold mercenary killer?

I hope you will enjoy the assassinations recounted in this book. They are factual. In assassination there is no need to indulge in fiction, for the very nature of assassination is that it has moved out of the context and background of ordinary life and ordinary living and entered a world which we might well believe was fictional unless we knew that all these strange and sinister crimes had actually taken place.

2

The Assassination of the Lord of Life

THERE is a delightful photograph, published some eighty years ago, by the *Illustrated London News,* which shows a diplomatic mission from King Chulalongkorn of Siam bearing a letter from the King to Queen Victoria and presenting themselves to the Queen at a ceremony at Windsor Castle.

The Siamese Ambassador, followed by four of his mandarins, has proceeded from the door of the Throne Hall on his knees. It was possible in the days of prostration for Siamese officials to move quite easily and with considerable speed in this posture. Old Siamese can still do it today. In the photograph the Ambassador has reached a point at the foot of the throne, and, without daring to raise his eyes directly towards the resplendent figure above him, he is reading a message from his own monarch. Just after the photograph was taken he handed up, with his left hand supported by his right hand, the King's letter to the Queen. He and his officials left the room as they had come, moving with remarkable agility on their knees over the castle floor.

Prostration no longer takes place in Siam except privately before the King and occasionally it is practised by old servants in private houses. In June 1932 a *coup d'état* took place in Bangkok which eventually substituted military dictatorship for the absolute rule of the monarch. But the King remained on his throne and the monarchy was retained in Siam. After the second world war the eyes of the Thai people turned to their young King Ananda, who had been educated in Switzerland. The Siamese people, although they had accepted the revolution as a fact, had never transferred their affection from the monarch to the dictator and it was clear that the prestige, if not the power, of the monarchy might quickly be revived by a prince who by his nature and good looks and by the dignity of his behaviour made an instant appeal to the Siamese people. Such a prince was Ananda, young, handsome, spontaneous with that innate dignity that has been a marked attribute of the successive kings of the Chakri dynasty during the last one hundred and sixty years.

I had just arrived at my office in the Ministry of Justice, immediately opposite the Grand Palace, when, a few minutes past nine o'clock on the morning of the 9th June 1946, a shot was heard coming from the King's bedchamber. I looked out of my window and saw a high palace official, whom I knew quite well, running in the greatest haste through the great Western Gate of the Palace. The sight was so unusual that I dropped my papers and walked over the road, passing through the gate unchallenged. The guard knew me because I was in the habit, from time to time, of walking round that part of the Palace that contained the Temple of the Emerald Buddha. Within the palace wall there was an atmosphere of such calm serenity that it was a delightful escape from the busy court over which, with my Siamese colleagues, I presided.

The King's mother and brother, who were hastily summoned, found the young King—he was only twenty—dead, killed by a bullet that had passed through his forehead and—as was later noticed—out of the back of his neck.

It is difficult for us to realise the shock caused to the Thai people by the death of their King. True, since 1932, the King of Siam had not been absolute. Since the revolution of that year he had exercised perhaps less direct political power than the Queen of England. Yet the Thai people still regarded the monarch as divine, the Teacher and the Protector of the Thai race, the representative of Buddha here on earth. The whole nation wept for their dead King.

I was so close to the events that preceded and followed the King's death that I am now able to write a frank and unbiased record of what happened. It is impossible to come to any judgment in the case without knowing at least the skeleton of the political events that led up to it.

For years after 1932 Thailand had been dominated by two men, Luang Pibul Songram, the Premier, and Luang Pradist Manudharm (Pridi Panomyong), whom, for short, we will call Nai Pridi. Pibul was a soldier of immense personal courage and charm. Nai Pridi was the son of a Thai father and a Chinese mother. At present he is in exile in Pekin. Pibul represented the right in Siam, Pridi the left.

During the war, when Thailand, occupied by Japanese troops, was forced into an alliance with Japan, Marshal Pibul carried on as premier, while Pridi was made regent, the young King, Ananda, being in Switzerland. From this vantage point Pridi organised the Free Thai movement and earned the gratitude of the Allies, which, as we shall see, was later to save his life.

As soon as the first two atom bombs had been dropped, the Japanese Emperor, through a flying emissary, ordered the surrender of the very large Japanese force, over five divisions, stationed in Thailand. General Slim, at the head of the victorious British and Indian troops, took the surrender. I released myself from Japanese imprisonment in time to see him do it.

My first birthday out of captivity fell on the 22nd January 1946. On that day I stood immediately behind the Supreme Allied Commander, Lord Louis Mountbatten, and the young King as the British war leader took the salute of the British troops who were shortly to leave Thailand, having done their job of shipping the Japanese army back to Japan.

The two men were in acute contrast. Mountbatten, middle-aged, already growing portly, stiffened into a figure of considerable dignity as he took the salute. He was not, I thought, a likable, irresistible personality like General 'Bill' Slim, but he had a commanding presence.

The young King was slim, almost delicate-looking in his white uniform and glasses, with a thoughtful and sensitive face. It was noticeable that the acclaim of the crowd was for the King alone. Mountbatten, the foreigner, was tolerated as the guest of the King. One could almost feel the hostility provoked by the parade of foreign troops on the Pramane ground, that great stretch of grass outside the palace walls where Simese kings are cremated, and where fairs are held.

The tension passed, or appeared to pass. The British left. The struggle for power between Pibul, who had resigned when the British came in, and Pridi, who had the support of the Navy and the Free Thai movement, began.

Pridi looked as if he might win the struggle until that fatal morning of the 9th of June.

Between the British review and his death I had seen King Ananda twice. He visited Chinatown and was accorded an ovation of extraordinary warmth by the Chinese, who thought, quite rightly, that he was the guarantor of the traditional Thai liberalism that had, for over a century, allowed foreigners to work their way to fortune and fame in Siam. A week later I had to fly to India on legal business. I returned the night of the Oxford and Cambridge Dinner in Bangkok, held in Prince Chumpot's palace, and attended by some sixty Thai and thirty Europeans. My plane was late and I arrived half-way through the dinner. To my dismay, as I entered, I saw the King's blue Rolls-Royce parked in the palace gates. I knew that arrangements must have been made for the King, who had taken the degree of Doctor of Law at Lausanne University, to attend the dinner. To arrive after the King was practically a capital offence. I entered the great dining hall looking desperately for a vacant seat. There was only one, almost opposite the King's chair. An equerry beckoned me to it. For the next two hours I was able to observe this young man. His quiet charm, gentleness and natural dignity were captivating. I felt sure that under his guidance Thailand would soon arise from the bitter ashes of the war years. The King left at eight minutes to eleven. In forty-eight hours he was dead.

When on the morning of June 9th it was known that the King was dead, confusion and grief enveloped the Palace. The Queen Mother was distraught and the King's brother, the present King, shocked and bewildered by the awful tragedy.

Pridi was Minister of the Royal Household at the time and under his direction two steps were taken that greatly increased the confusion in the Palace, the turmoil in the nation, and lessened the chances of discovering who the real murderer was.

A communiqué was issued to the public stating that the King had been indisposed for a week, and that he had died on the morning of the 9th. 'It is believed death was due to an accident which happened while the King was handling a revolver.'

This statement raised a storm of protest throughout the nation. The King's indisposition had been a mild constipation for which he had taken an aperient. He was in good health and full of the love of life. The people just did not believe the innuendo of suicide contained in the official statement. Nor did they believe that the King, who was an expert on firearms, had had an accident with his revolver. The people believed that for some dark and sinister motive which they could not unravel, evil men had murdered the King.

When the course of events during the morning of June 9th became known the public outcry intensified.

Ministers and the great princes had been summoned to the Palace on that morning, but they had been kept waiting more than two hours. During that time nearly all the essential evidence in the case had been removed. The body of the King had been washed and laid out on a bed in an adjoining room. His revolver, which had been found at his side and on his bed, had been handled by a number of people. All that the Ministers could see was a blackened bullet hole high in the King's forehead over the left eye.

Even then no one dared to suggest an autopsy. The persons of the Thai kings were still sacred. It was probably the reluctance of the Thai doctors to touch the royal person that had led to the death of King Vachiravudya. The tradition was not easily broken.

Pibul and his followers would have been less than human if they had not striven to improve their position as a result of the awful calamity that had befallen Pridi and his associates. The Pibul faction was at that time being taunted with accusations of collaboration with the Japanese. Here was a crime far greater in Thai eyes, and for it the Pridi party must be held responsible. This was the line that the opposition took, and it led directly to Pibul's return to power, and to Pridi fleeing the country a hunted exile at the end of 1947.

Meanwhile Pridi had set up Royal Commissions of enquiry that achieved nothing at all.[1] A mixed commission of doctors, British and Indian, as well as Thai, did, however, declare that the original communiqué had been mistaken. The King's death, the doctors announced, might have been due to an accident or even suicide, but murder could not be precluded. This made Pridi's position even more untenable.

Under the old regime his ministerial responsibility, as opposed to personal implication in the crime, would have been absolute. Ancient custom would not have allowed the Minister of the Royal Household to survive the murder of his master whose care was his special concern.

It so happened that I was fated to see this drama played out to its end. Pridi was cornered in his house at Ta Prachan, but that house was well chosen. The garden at

1. In the end there were two such commissions. Neither achieved any concrete or helpful result.

the rear faces the Menam, the great Bangkok river. As Pibul's men battered on the locked gates of the outer buildings Pridi slipped across the river by sampan. He took refuge with the navy, who controlled the opposite bank, and stayed there under cover for some days. Then one of the oddest pieces of British diplomacy ever enacted was staged. Pridi was a personal friend of Captain Dennis, the British Naval Attaché in Bangkok. Captain Dennis was a sailor of courage and resource. He was also a loyal friend to those who had helped Britain in the war. In a secret cloak-and-dagger operation, with the connivance of the British authorities, Pridi was smuggled down the Menam river, fifteen miles, to the sea in a fast motor launch. The launch passed under the guarding guns at Paknam at the river mouth. Pridi was placed safely on board a British merchantman and three days later was in Singapore.

The following week I was in Singapore conducting two legal cases in the city. I walked into the Thai Consulate to receive my return visas to Bangkok. As I stood waiting, Pridi himself walked in. The stocky figure, the hair *en brosse*, the large penetrating eyes, were instantly recognisable. He had been temporarily—and comfortably— interned by the authorities. He had come to receive his mail, and the Thai newspapers. No official of the Consulate dared to speak to him. A junior clerk handed him his mail in silence.

As he was leaving he turned to me to ask when I was returning. I said the following day.

He smiled: 'I can't—not yet. Perhaps some day. *Au revoir.*'

He was gone.

A month later he had found his way to China, his shadow still heavy over Siam. Once only, since then, did he visit his own country. Disguised as a naval officer, in a coup that failed, he penetrated the Grand Palace and took control for some hours of the very apartments the King had been murdered in.

The political drama that ended in November 1947 with the return of Pibul to power and the exile of Pridi Panomyong tended to overshadow any careful and painstaking investigation of the crime. On this subject a great deal of biased conjecture has been printed in Britain. Very often it is clear that the writers just do not know the facts completely and are unfamiliar with their background. I take the following comment in an article in the *New Statesman and Nation*, a paper renowned for its accuracy as well as for its literary distinction:

'Is accident excluded? That the commission of enquiry should decide that no one could be accidentally shot in the forehead at such close range as to blacken the skin seems at first quite reasonable. But such an accident is not excluded. The story had been reconstructed in the following manner. At seven o'clock the King had been dosed with castor oil and had stayed in bed waiting events. It would be in accordance with his usual habit to load his revolver with the idea of bird-shooting. He would be interrupted by the necessity of hurrying into his bathroom. After his return, he would naturally feel inclined to lie down. He may have dozed, awakening soon afterwards to remember that he had left his revolver loaded and cocked by his bedside. Being very well accustomed to firearms, he would feel he ought to unload it and lazily stretch out his left hand for it without getting up. In that case the revolver, in his left hand, would have passed directly over his head on its way to his right hand. If the revolver slipped, he would have clutched it tightly, and it is, on this reconstruction, perfectly possible to imagine the trigger being pulled and the bullet entering his head high in his forehead. This, of course, is again mere hypothesis, but it offers a plausible example of how such an accident could take place.'[1]

1. I was informed by the senior British doctor on the panel that was finally authorised to hold an autopsy that the direction and trajectory of the bullet precluded suicide and made accident highly improbable.

What is not mentioned here is the fact that it is quite possible that the King was not killed with his .45 Colt revolver but by another weapon, and that no spasm whatever was found in the King's hand as would be expected if he himself had pulled the trigger. Moreover, those who knew the King knew beyond argument that he was the last young man likely to take his own life, and that his mastery and understanding of firearms was complete.

When Pibul assumed power three men were arrested. Two were royal pages (Nai Chitra and Nai Butr, described in the British Press as 'faithful aristocrats') and Nai Chalow, a secretary and henchman of Pridi. When, years later, all three were executed by shooting, Chalow survived the first fusillade, and died slowly. The two pages fell at once. Whatever may have been the opinion of foreign newspaper men there is no doubt that the execution of these men, regarded as the actual murderers, as opposed to the instigators, was welcomed by the entire Thai people. They felt that the death of their King had at last been avenged.

There still remains the greatest and most fascinating problem of all. Who were the real murderers, the men who said: 'This man must die'?

The final decision of the doctors favoured by a majority assassination as the cause of death. But the secretary and the two pages were not the men to instigate so terrible and awful a crime. They may well have been the men to carry it out. Chalow, whom I knew slightly, was a sinister, heavy, brooding figure who seemed to be for ever pondering some dark mystery. The two pages were neither of them men who should have been solely entrusted with the safety of the King. Yet all three are obviously small fry.

After twenty-five years of intimate experience of Thailand and the Far East I must attribute the death of King Ananda to a Communist plot. Consider the situation. The fact and idea of monarchy, once all-powerful in the Far East, had been smashed nearly everywhere. In India the British government was to betray the maharajahs with

whom we had solemn treaties of friendship. In Malaya
the princes were in fact controlled by their British advisers. In Sumatra and Java the kings had to give way to
popular government. By an act of great folly, as far back
as the eighties, the British had destroyed the Burmese
monarchy that could have been so useful and powerful an
ally. In China itself the last Empress was but a memory,
and Communism was soon to be in the saddle. Only in
Siam the idea of kingship remained inviolate. As long as
there was a king in Thailand, a Communist dictatorship
was unthinkable.

The case for a foul dark Communist coup to remove
the King was, to the Communists, a political necessity.
There was, in fact, no other way in which Communism
in Siam could achieve its aims. The standard of living
in Siam was rising year by year. The country had an unsinkable rice economy with thousands of tons of export-
able surplus. The Siamese peasant-farmer, as a rule, owns
his land. Even the large Chinese community, which might
be expected to support a Communist regime on national
grounds, had rallied solidly round the King, as had been
shown by the extraordinary expressions of love and devotion on the occasion of the royal visit to the Chinese
merchants and people. In Thailand, the key to the Far
East, the gateway to great riches and power in Malaya,
Burma, India and Indonesia, the Communists had little
hope of achieving their ambitions. The longer they delayed, the less chance there was of their ambitions ever
being realised.

Against this background my reconstruction of this baf-
fling crime would be far different from the reconstruction
I have already quoted. I, too, find the police evidence
and the reports of the two Royal Commissions inconclu-
sive, biased and unsatisfactory. But I am convinced that
as soon as British troops left Siam, the Japanese having
been deported, the Communist Party decided to take
over in Siam. It could only do this by creating the utmost confusion. The King's death would cause this as

nothing else would. The King's younger brother might well be frightened from ever returning to Thailand once he was back in the security of Switzerland, where, like his brother, he went to school. It was indeed a glittering prize. Siam had suffered four years of Japanese occupation, six months of a tolerant, but objectionable, British occupation. If a stable, strong government were to achieve power the opportunity would be for ever lost.

In the dark ill-lit back room of a Chinese house the leaders of Communism in Thailand, who had no following, but great ambition, met each week. There the murder was plotted. Great rewards were held out to the two, or possibly three, leading Thais who shared the awful secret. On the evening of the 8th the murderer was secreted in the royal bedchamber. While the King was still asleep in the morning he shot the King at point-blank range through the forehead. The bullet was later found embedded in the mattress under the King's left elbow. A shot during the night would have given the whole treacherous plot away. Then it would have been murder with accident precluded. Besides, the door of the bedoom was guarded outside, until dawn. In the early morning the murderer was able to slip out and himself break the news of the King's death. That is how Ananda died.

The only happy circumstance of this great tragedy was that the perpetrators did not achieve their purpose. They under-estimated the immediate universal fury of the Thai people with those who, they suspected, had killed their King. Pibul was able to ride to power on the wave of popular anger and resentment.

In a quiet bungalow, in the suburbs of Pekin, Nai Pridi, still an exile, contemplates the vicissitudes of political fortune. But he remembered his friend Captain Dennis, who now has a silver cigarette box inscribed: 'A friend in need is a friend indeed.'

The present young King of Siam, His Majesty King Bhumipol Adulej, reigns in his brother's stead. He has married a beautiful queen, the daughter of a former Ambassador in London. He has a son and heir, born on July 28th, 1952. So the great conception of Eastern monarchy lives on in Siam. The King is dead, but the new King reigns. The Siamese people, alone of the people of the Far East, when they tire of the wiles of politicians, can still say: 'Our teacher and protector is with us. Our Lord lives.'

The black, evil crime of regicide, the calculated murder of King Ananda casts its shadow over Thailand, but to this day the King and the people are still one, children of the great teacher, Buddha, himself.

The assassination of King Ananda remains, in some respects, the greatest mystery of modern time. Almost certainly we have not been told the whole story. It may well be that the forces of Communism originating in China and determined to extend their influence as far as India, thought, immediately after the second world war, that they could achieve this great extension of their empire to the rich, warm rice-producing countries of the south by stealth and subversion. They did not contemplate, at that time, that they would be met by force as in Korea and Vietnam. The plans for a take-over by disruption and by murder failed but it must have looked at the time as if they might succeed and it is, I think, this background that explains the horrible killing of the young King whose personality and gifts held out so much promise for the monarchy and the Siamese people.

3

The Feud

LEON TROTSKY, whose real name was Lev Davidovitch Bronstein, was born at Yanovka in the Ukraine. He was the son of a prosperous Jewish farmer and of a Jewish mother. His revolutionary activities seemed to have started as soon as he left school, possibly before, and at the age of twenty-one, in 1900, we find him being exiled to Siberia for dangerous revolutionary activity directed against the Czarist regime. He escaped from Siberia and found his way abroad, which enabled him to take part in the Russian Social Democratic Party Conference of 1903. He returned to St. Petersburg in 1905, became President of the St. Petersburg Revolutionary Soviet, but was unable to escape the sharp eyes of the police, who again arrested him. By now he was becoming something of an escape expert and he managed to escape a second time from Siberia and to circumvent all the difficulties entailed by a marked man leaving Russia. Later we find him in Vienna, in Madrid and in New York. He returned to Russia in 1917 and was promptly imprisoned by the Provisional Government. Then he joined the Bolsheviks. He was the leader of the Petrograd Soviet during the revolutionary months and again became their president.

Leon Trotsky was perhaps the best brain among the Soviet revolutionary leaders. He stood out head and shoulders above the rank and file of the immense party leadership. It was only natural that he should be made

Commissar for Foreign Affairs to lead the Russian delegation at Brest-Litovsk. Nor was his war record ever in doubt, for from 1918 to 1925, as Commissar for War, he controlled and inspired the revolutionary army during the vital years of the civil war. From 1920 onwards he wrote a number of books and pamphlets all of which developed the theme that revolution in Russia could not be fully developed or exploited unless other countries in the West joined the Soviet Union in overthrowing their reactionary regimes. This was the summit of his career, for the more prominent he became the more respected he was, the more he incurred the hatred of Joseph Vissarionovich Stalin, who had been born in the same year as Trotsky in the town of Gori, Georgia, the son of a poverty-stricken cobbler recently freed from serfdom, who was to become his deadly rival.

Trotsky was too big a man to be demoted in one blow. In the Russian manner with which we have become so familiar, from 1925 onwards he held only second-rank posts and it took two years to expel him from the party at the end of 1927. He managed to leave Russia to live in exile in France. For a short while he stayed in Norway and then he left for Mexico, where the government extended hospitality to him and he was able to live in peace with his family.

However, the intense jealousy and hatred that had poisoned the long relationship between Stalin and Trotsky never died. Joseph Stalin was a complete contrast to Trotsky. Whereas Trotsky excelled in putting into words the rhyme and rhythm of the revolution, inspiring the masses with his oratory, Stalin spoke very little. During the civil war Stalin was much closer to the actual revolutionary organisation but he was subject to the overall direction of Trotsky as War Minister. It was during this time that the two men, totally different in temperament and coming from different worlds, began to irritate each other unbearably.

Trotsky, the intellectual, was immensely interested in

the philosophy of revolution. Stalin was dedicated to the mechanics of power which led in the mid-thirties to the ruthless arrests and staged trials designed to suppress all opposition. Stalin was building up a great ruling party which he controlled through Beria, his police chief. The vast peasant population of Russia was exploited and almost returned to the serfdom they had known fifty years before. The political purges went on and on and were far more ruthless and far more 'undemocratic' than anything the Czars had ever thought of, or the emperors of China had ever conceived.

Stalin started to build up his image as the father figure of all the Russians. In effect he became a revolutionary Czar. From his austere, gleamingly white, private apartments he ruled the great world of Russia and even the highest party leaders went in dread of incurring his displeasure.

So it came about, within quite a short period, that no criticism of Stalin was ever heard in Russia and Stalin became used to the climate of implicit obedience and even adulation, which he despised. He had not forgotten Trotsky. Trotsky saw to that. Stalin had now, in the public estimation, inherited the purple cloak of Lenin as the protector of Marxist doctrine and the traditions of the revolution. No one in the Soviet Union dared to write or to speak one word of criticism or of denigration. But Trotsky, now living in Mexico, never stopped writing and his writings found their way by subterranean means into the Soviet Union. He pulled to pieces the whole beautiful picture of the man of steel who was Lenin's natural heir, the depositary of all revolutionary wisdom. Instead he pictured Stalin as a sly and unscrupulous wire-puller without political convictions because he lacked the intellect to grasp the essentials of revolutionary philosophy.

There was enough truth in this picture to make Stalin murderously angry. He could not afford to allow his reputation to be undermined in this way. At the Moscow trials between 1936 and 1938 Stalin did his best to blacken the name of Trotsky for ever in the eyes of all Russians. The prosecution alleged that Trotsky had co-operated with Nazi Germany through Rudolf Hess in plans to overthrow the Soviet Union and to restore capitalism in Russia. Stalin knew, of course, that this was a gigantic lie, but there is a principle in international politics which says that the bigger the lie the better. It is more difficult to kill a big lie than a little lie, for the big lie, by its nature, tears out the roots of truth and may itself in time become firmly planted in the minds of a great many people.

Stalin and Trotsky were now five thousand miles apart, sniping at each other with their poisoned darts, Trotsky hoping one day to return and to be acclaimed by the revolution which he had led and loved, Stalin fearful lest one day he should see that bearded, unmistakable figure springing up the steps towards the inner chambers of the Kremlin. The hatred that Stalin had for Trotsky was the primitive hatred of the peasant who never lost his tribal instincts nor his inclination towards a passionate vendetta. Stalin always regretted that he had not had Trotsky murdered during the two years when he was gradually being deprived of power. It would have been so easy. That destructive sneering pen would never have been able to write again. The Stalin legend would have had but one version. And there is some ground for thinking that Stalin hated Trotsky because, although he had deprived him of power, Trotsky, in exile, appeared to be a happier figure than the morose Georgian master of Russia. Stalin had never been able to get on reasonably well with his wives. His first wife, Katherine Svanidze, died three years after he married her in 1904. The son of this marriage was said to have been killed by the Nazis in 1944. His next wife, Nadezhda Allilueva, who bore him a son and a daughter, was said to have committed suicide, but there is at least a suspicion that Stalin murdered her. A third marriage followed with Rosa Kaganovich, but this was followed very quickly by divorce. It seems that the man who had murdered his way to power was personally a most unhappy and frustrated man.

This, then, is a case of epic hatred. At first Stalin thought that Trotsky was a cross that he would have to bear until he or Trotsky died, and then the thought occurred to him: Why should not Trotsky die first? Stalin had been able to pursue two or three of his dangerous minor enemies abroad and murder them in France, in Turkey and even in Egypt. Would it not be possible to murder Leon Trotsky in Mexico? It would be a formidable enterprise. It would need the most careful planning. It was known that Trotsky was guarded night and day by men devoted to his person. Stalin pondered this matter in his heart and his cunning Georgian brain came up with the answer. Either the murder could be achieved by a sudden swift assault by armed men who might rush the guards if they stormed into the house at night, or, if this failed, it might be possible to infiltrate the assassin into the house itself, so that Stalin's agent would be quite unsuspected by Trotsky and gradually gain his confidence, after which the murder of his detested enemy would be a matter of one strong murderous blow.

The murder of Trotsky is so glaring an example of the long vengeful arm of Communist hatred and the obsession of one man to kill another that it must surely rank as one of the world's great assassinations.

Trotsky's life reads like a tale from the *Arabian Nights*. He attended school and the university in Odessa, and was first convicted of revolutionary activity when he was twenty-one. The sentence? East Siberia. After three years of privation, during which he learnt to stand pain, whether induced by the whips of the Czarist police or by the cold, he escaped not only from Russia but from the Continent. In 1902 he calmly enters Britain, via the Port of London, bearing a forged passport in the false name of Leon Trotsky. His success made him attached to his new name. He bore it till he died.

In London he collaborated with Lenin and Plekhanev

in editing a Communist newspaper. But he was young and did not relish exile. He boldly returned to Russia to become chairman of the St. Petersburg Council of Workers' Deputies. It was in fact a Soviet. At a meeting, with Trotsky in the chair, the whole meeting, including women, was arrested. Siberia was the inevitable sentence. Trotsky escaped almost as soon as he got there. He had become complete master of the cloak-and-dagger technique. As soon as he crossed the border, he settled in Vienna to work for *Pravda*. He was a writer by profession and instinct.

During the 1914–18 war his book *Origins of the War* was published in German. It brought him eight months' imprisonment. When he had served this sentence—one of the few not cut short by his own initiative and daring—he made his way to France. He was expelled, and crossed the border into Spain, where he was arrested for illegal entry, but allowed, later, to leave for the United States. He was in New York editing *The New World* when in 1917 the Russian revolution broke at last. Immediately he wanted to return, but was delayed by being arrested by the British in Halifax, Nova Scotia.

It was not until the middle of July, four months after the first uprising, that he reached the Russian capital. He became a Bolshevik party member the same month, took over the direction of affairs jointly with Lenin, and, as the People's Commissar for Foreign Affairs, negotiated the Peace Treaty of Brest-Litovsk.

When the organisation of a new army to defeat the White Russians became of paramount importance he moved to the Ministry of War. With the help of a large number of former Czarist officers he was almost solely responsible for laying the foundations of the Red Army.

On Lenin's death his position seemed assured as Russian leader. It was not. Lenin had said of Stalin: 'This cook makes too strong a stew.' But Stalin, the party secretary, with Zinoviev, plotted and planned and eventually was able to expel Trotsky from the party. That was in

1927. From that date Trotsky's immense vision was lost to the leaders of Soviet Russia. Gradually the coarse, limited, ruthless Stalin tightened his grip until the time came when to disagree with him was death.

Many of the Russian leaders disagreed with him. Many died.

Meanwhile Leon Trotsky had made his way to Constantinople, but he was looking for a permanent home. Britain and America, discreditably, I feel, refused him visas. Only Mexico would issue him with a visa—and the necessary foreigner's resident papers as well. Lazaro Cardenas, a man who combined dictatorship with certain surprisingly liberal impulses, was premier of Mexico. Trotsky wrote to thank him for the hospitality and generosity shown by the Mexican government.

In Moscow, Stalin, growing daily more powerful, had started to murder his opponents quite systematically by every stratagem of deceit and treachery. Blood apparently increased his appetite, for the first solitary murders were soon to develop into the purges, the mass judicial murders, with the horrible craven judges and mad, doped, cringing prisoners. Only one man was outside Stalin's power. Or was he? Stalin pondered the matter. There is some evidence that his original plan was to kidnap Trotsky and bring him back to the Soviet Union. That, of course, would have been much more satisfying. He could have been left to rot for a year or two in semi-darkness, then, broken, brought out into the light and made to confess. The confession would say that he had been in league with capitalist leaders. He would be made to beg for his life. The whole technique, whereby the prisoner whose brain is changed by torture and suggestion becomes a cringing masochistic creature full of self-accusation, would have its finest flowering with Trotsky as the victim. But this was not to happen. His agents told Stalin it was impossible to bring Trotsky alive to the Soviet Union. If he was to die, Stalin had no use for his corpse. He might as well die in exile in Mexico. And so it was arranged.

Anyone who studies the fantastic remote-control murder of Leon Trotsky agrees that every line of evidence, every tendril of fact and circumstance, leads from the murdered man's study in Mexico straight to the arch-murderer in Moscow: to Stalin himself.

The motive for the crime was clear. Stalin could not afford to let Trotsky live. Trotsky alone had the knowledge, authority and means to tell the world what Stalin really was. And he was going to do so: he had completed his life of Lenin. He was making a draft of his life of Stalin. Had it been written and published, the Stalin myth would have been exploded fifteen years before Marshal Bulganin and Mr. Khrushchev tore the veil away.

Trotsky was a visionary, but a practical one. He did not lie around in the Mexican sun waiting for the blow to fall. In the pleasant suburb of Coyoacan he built one of the most remarkable houses in Mexico City. It was flat, T-shaped, and from the outside resembled a prison—or a fortress—which was just what it was. There were three machine-gun towers manned by Trotsky's henchmen, a system of external electric lights which could reveal any visitor as he approached, and a main door that was a masterpiece of ingenuity. The craftsmen and the electricians had worked upon it so that it was impossible even to approach it without raising an alarm and becoming completely visible, at night as well as by day, to the guards inside.

Inside the house was the garden—a plan adopted now by the most modern young architects—and Trotsky's chief pleasure was to walk amongst the very rare cacti and other Mexican flowers, which included a complete night garden. Stalin was not deterred by these elaborate precautions. On the 24th May 1940 he struck. Twenty armed men fired more than two hundred shots into the house. They were beaten off believing that they had done the job, killing Trotsky in the fusilade. That remarkably tough and agile man had sprung into a prepared alcove in a bedroom wall and escaped. His wife, Nathalie Sedova, and his small grandchild also escaped death.

The head of the Mexican police was soon on the scene, much perturbed, for by this time the President had started to take quite a pride in the preservation of Trotsky in spite of all the Communist murder squads could contrive. Yet the police chief was not, at first, sure that the attack had not been faked by Trotsky himself. This extraordinary idea was apparently encouraged by the fact that Trotsky and his family were calm immediately after the attempted murder. The Mexican police thought this most suspicious. It does not seem to have occurred to them that after a life of more than ordinary vicissitude Leon Trotsky was becoming a fatalist, but a fatalist who, nevertheless, took what precautions were in his power.

After this first attack several improvements were carried out in what we should now call the security aspects of the house. A ledge outside the Trotsky bedroom window was sawn off. A new system of wires that electrocuted was devised for the outer wall, and the guards were instructed to scrutinise visitors more carefully. 'If he cannot penetrate from outside, he will strike from inside,' said Trotsky. He knew Stalin's mind. Five thousand miles away he could read the cunning twisted mind of the Georgian. He read it with absolute accuracy.

It is still not clear how the man who called himself Jacson managed to ingratiate himself so quickly into the Trotsky household. One account says that he first contacted friends of Trotsky who were bringing his grandson from France to join Trotsky and his wife. If this was so, it may have accounted for the fact that Trotsky seems never to have entertained any suspicion of Jacson. The guards, for some reason, did not like him, but he was their master's friend. They had to admit him.

Trotsky was an inveterate writer. His works, read today, reveal an eagle vision and catholic lack of bigotry. He understood that revolutions were dealing in the hearts of men. Jacson took it upon himself to help Trotsky in his work. He was diligent and intelligent. Trotsky found him very useful. Trotsky did not know that Jacson took his orders direct from the central committee of the Communist party, that is from Stalin. By August Jacson had visited Trotsky ten times, and become his confidant. Stalin, in the Kremlin, gave the signal: 'Kill him.'

On the afternoon of the 20th August Trotsky, as usual, was writing at his desk. Jacson was announced and Trotsky greeted him. Trotsky had great charm and simplicity of manner. Although not without vanity, he seemed to be genuinely interested in everyone, important or otherwise. Jacson handed the seated figure at the desk some proofs. Trotsky nodded, and thanked him. The clear Mexican sunshine poured in through the window, lighting up the remarkable features of the man at the desk, his pointed beard which the cartoonists had seized on, the high forehead, and the great sad eyes that seemed to reflect the world's sorrow.

Jacson withdrew, but was back in a few moments. This time, knowing who it was, and trusting him completely, immersed in his work, Trotsky did not even look up. Jacson moved behind the seated figure at the desk bent over his papers. He stood by a small table pretending to file some documents. He drew from inside his coat an axe. He raised it high above his head until the sun caught its blade in a wicked gleam. Trotsky made to turn round as the axe was brought down deep into his skull. The blood spurted from the wound, staining the white papers on the desk red.

Trotsky's wife Nathalie, as if sensing some dread occurrence, came in. She flung herself round her husband. The murderer was seized. Trotsky was not yet dead.

His wife bandaged him, tried to reassure him.

'It is no good, dear,' he said. 'This time he has done it. I die. I love you.'

The vicious little rat of a man who had perpetrated this horrible crime could utter only five words, but they were significant. When charged his reply was: 'They made me do it.'

The second world war came to prevent full meaning of the murder of Leon Trotsky being appreciated. Years later we were to understand that Joseph Stalin lived on murder as ordinary men live on bread.

The murder of Trotsky, so far from obliterating his influence, greatly increased it. His memory became enshrined and his works were read much more widely and more carefully than they would have been otherwise. Followers who believed in his brand of philosophic revolution were and are to be found in many countries. Stalin, after the murder, became even more taciturn and had the air of a stricken man. Perhaps in some unexpressed way he felt that he had killed a brother revolutionary and that in murdering Trotsky he had murdered something of the Russian revolution, its flame perhaps, the torch by which it might have led the world. What was left? Only a drab monolithic materialistic state struggling to achieve enough for the people to eat and to wear and enough houses to shelter them. The prophet of the revolution was dead and the whole world knew that Stalin was his murderer. From this moment onwards millions of people who had been attracted by the basic idealism of the Soviet revolution lost faith in it. Stalin not only murdered Trotsky. He killed much more than one man. The spirit of the Russian revolution was never to be the same again.

4

The American Way of Death

DALLAS is the heart of Texas and Texas is not like any other American state. It is a huge area divided into no less than two hundred and fifty-four counties.

Texas, of course, was until comparatively recently an outlying province of the Spanish American empire. The Louisiana Purchase in 1803 brought the United States into direct contact with Spanish-held territory. As late as 1819 the Florida Treaty with Spain fixed the Sabine and Red rivers as the boundary between the United States and Mexico. Early attempts by the United States to buy Texas from Mexico failed, but the Mexican authorities allowed and even encouraged American immigration into their country.

Friction arose between the American immigrants and the Mexican government partly because the Americans thought that the Mexican officials were corrupt and unpredictable, as indeed they were, and partly because the American immigrants insisted on keeping their slaves which, rather remarkably, was a serious offence under Mexican law. The bad feeling between the American immigrants and the Mexican authorities was made much worse by the arrival of a type of immigrant who was in fact an armed adventurer prepared to shoot his way, if possible, to riches. An open breach came in 1835 when Santa-Anna brought in a constitution doing away with all state rights and proclaiming the Lone Star republic independent of Mexico. This was followed by a war of exceptional brutality in which very few prisoners were taken and in 1837 the United States recognised the new republic. The Mexican war of 1846, which lasted nearly two years, followed until in 1870 Congress recognised the legal status of the Texas government which had hitherto been a *de facto* ruling body.

I have set out this very brief description of the genesis of Texas to show that it is less than one hundred years since the Texas matter was finally settled. Spain, incidentally, and, of course, Mexico, has not given up her claim to the conquered territory. What emerges is the unique history of Texas which was to breed a special type of American. It took a long time for the West to become domesticated. The American war with the Indian tribes lasted nearly a hundred years, but once the American Indians had been subjugated and confined to reservations, peace came to the West and the Americans who opened up the West became farmers.

The same tradition was not followed in Texas. The tradition of sudden death in Texas survives until the present time. Because of this, murder is regarded in a completely different light. The city of Dallas is still notorious for its annual crop of murders, both those which the police discover and the far great number which, for one reason or another, are never made the subject of court proceedings. There are many things which the United States do better than the long-civilised European countries but there are two exceptions to this. The first is the American judicial system, which is hopelessly inefficient and outdated, and the second is the police force, which, until recently at any rate, has been notoriously corrupt. The defects of the American judicial system, which include dilatory procedures which defeat justice, also comprises American judicial investigations, which are far less independent and outspoken than similar investigations in Britain. Americans themselves complain that the type of man who is attracted to the law in America and is likely to receive judicial preferment is regrettably low as compared with most European countries.

In spite of all this Texas might have remained a comparatively normal state in which reasonable law and order was contained had it not been for the fantastic explosion of oil wealth. This swift and sudden rise from poverty to great riches was unique even in the development of the American continent. It led to the emergence of a race of men who, by their initiative, daring, cunning and ruthlessness, had clawed their way to the top and who were determined that no one, ever, should interfere with their way of life.

This is the real background to the assassination of John Fitzgerald Kennedy at 12.30 p.m. on a beautiful day, November 22nd 1963, while on a visit to Dallas.

The presidential motorcade was on its way to take the President to lunch. It turned right into Houston Street, passed the County Criminal Court and the County Records Building and entered Elm Street. Before the presidential car, which was surrounded by a police escort, had reached the tripple under-pass some two hundred yards ahead the President had received two wounds, one of which blew a great deal of his brains out of his skull. A bullet which was said to have gone through the President later hit Governor John B. Connally in the wrist and hand. The President was rushed to hospital, but he had been mortally wounded and he died.

A judicial enquiry was appointed, led by Chief Justice Warren and known to all the world as the Warren Commission. The Warren Commission has published twenty-six volumes of evidence, which included three thousand, one hundred and fifty-four exhibits, twenty-five thousand F.B.I. interviews and a great mass of detail. When it was all over Chief Justice Warren handed his report to President Johnson, who, of course, had been Vice-President under President Kennedy and who, therefore, automatically stepped into his shoes.

The murder of President Kennedy stunned and shocked the world. Perhaps never before had so many nations centred their hopes for a peaceful and prosperous life so fixedly on one comparatively young man. John Kennedy represented not only the people of the United States in their more idealistic mood, he also reflected the deep feeling that millions of men and women of all races had who believed that neither Fascism nor Communism, both brutal creeds, provided the answer to the future. It was Kennedy's brand of enlightened liberalism that made his star shine so brightly. He had shown in the Cuba crisis that he was capable of bold and realistic decision. The combination of idealist and man of action had an extraordinary world-wide appeal. At the same time there was no doubt whatever that deeply entrenched reactionary vested interest in the United States, and in Texas in particular, hated Kennedy and all he stood for. One would have thought, therefore, this being the background to this atrocious murder, that the Warren Commission would have spent a great deal of its time in probing the motive for this murder. In fact, it devoted nearly all its energy towards establishing a theory of the facts that would quieten the clamour that was growing in the United States after the public had recovered from the first appalling shock and the sinister speculation in the world Press.

Briefly, the basic conclusion of the Warren Commission was that President Kennedy was murdered by a man, Lee Harvey Oswald, who was acting alone. Oswald was said to have killed the President with a single bullet fired from a window in the Texas School Book Depository that overlooked Elm Street. Oswald, of course, was arrested and presumably was about to be tried for murder. At any rate, he was in police custody.

When the conclusions of the Warren Commission were published the American Press accepted them with some sombre reservations. The European Press and, in particular, the French Press came out with a derisive condemnation of the whole procedure. The British Press, which was much more restrained, was inclined to accept the report of the Warren Commission but pointed out that the conclusions seemed to leave wide gaps for speculation.

There has been considerable pressure directed towards the reopening of the whole case and it now seems certain that world opinion, at any rate, will not be satisfied until this is done. It is known that many of the chief figures who were in the motorcade at that time, as well as many members of the public who were present, disagree entirely with the findings of the Warren Commission, and these dissenters include Governor Connally and the widow of the dead President. Why is it that the findings of the Warren Commission, which were so prolonged and painstaking, are now regarded by wide sections of public opinion throughout the world as being an attempt to bury the real answers for ever so that those who planned the murder of John Kennedy will never be known? A number of books have been written—and very good books some of them are—exploring all the evidence and attempting to assess its validity or its worthlessness, but I have not seen any short summary of the case against the conclusions of the Warren Commission. As it might be very interesting to put the case against the Commission's findings in a compact form, I will now try to do this and the reader can then form his or her own conclusions as to whether the findings of the Warren Commission are credible or not. There is, of course, a school of thought which says that, regardless of whether the Warren Commission has arrived at the truth, it would be wrong to raise this whole matter again. President Kennedy is dead. Nothing can bring him to life again. Let him rest in peace. This is a view which I respect but entirely disagree with. If, in fact, the findings of the Warren Commission are incredible or so doubtful as to be suspect, then an immense effort should be made to get at the truth regardless of politics and regardless of the individuals who are deeply concerned. The case against the Warren Commission consists of a number of charges, some of them gen-

eral in character, but many of them highly specific. I will
set them out and number them for the sake of clarity and,
I hope, cogency.

(1) The Warren Commission was made up of men not
    sufficiently divorced from American political pres-
    sures. No one doubts the good faith of the Chief
    Justice, but the system whereby American judicial
    officers owe their appointments largely to political
    patronage makes all such commissions in the United
    States far less strong than they should be.

(2) The Warren Commission, guided by its terms of
    reference, devoted nearly all its energy and industry
    to the question: Who shot Kennedy? It devoted
    remarkably little time to the far more important
    question of determining whether there was a group
    of men who had planned this murder and who, of
    course, were themselves guilty of murder. As it was
    well known that John Kennedy had stubborn and
    bitter enemies in the state of Texas and in the city of
    Dallas in particular, one would have thought that
    this question of unmasking the real murderers would
    have consumed a great deal of the Commission's
    time.

(3) The Commission came out in favour of the theory
    that Oswald alone shot the President dead with a
    single bullet. The testimony of those who were
    present would appear to throw the gravest doubt
    on this theory. Governor Connally himself gave evi-
    dence that he was not hit by the bullet that hit the
    President but by another shot that was fired later.
    This is what he said:

    'Well, in my judgment it just could not have con-
    ceivably been the first one because I heard the sound
    of a shot. In the first place I don't know anything
    about the velocity of this particular bullet but any
    rifle has a velocity that exceeds the speed of sound,
    and when I heard the sound of that first shot, that
    bullet had already reached where I was. I had time

to turn to my right and start to turn to my left before
I felt anything. It is not conceivable to me that I
could have been hit by the first bullet.'

(4) The single-bullet theory which is the core of the
Warren Commission case is also negatived by the
almost unmarked condition of the bullet itself. Bullets that penetrate one body and then pass through
bone and muscle in another body are deeply marked.
This bullet was hardly marked at all. So that if we
accept the evidence of Governor Connally that there
were at least two shots—some spectators said there
was a fusilade of shots—then we must agree with
Norman Redlich, the Warren Commission lawyer,
who drafted a great deal of the Report, when he
said: 'To say that they were hit by separate bullets
is synonymous with saying there were two assassins.'

(5) The theory that Oswald alone executed the murder
from his window high up in the depository building
would certainly make him marksman of the year.
If, in fact, he was in the window at all and if he was
using the rifle attributed to him, then he was firing
at a small moving target in the street far below him
with a Mannleicher-Carcano Italian rifle made
about 1940. This rifle had originally been bought for
about twelve dollars. It is not possible to reload it
automatically. It is a most clumsy weapon and between each shot the bolt handle on the breach
mechanism has to be released, it has to be drawn
back to eject the spent cartridge, it has to be driven
forward to pick up a fresh cartridge from the magazine, and finally the bolt handle has to be re-locked.

(6) Although the Warren Commission decided that the
murder had been done by Oswald from the depository window, the consensus of opinion among the
public was that the shots did not come from the
window, or did not come exclusively from the window, but they came from a high grass verge near a

tree adjacent to a car park, just above and very close to the spot where the presidential car passed on its way down Elm Street. If we are dealing here with probabilities, certainly a shot or shots from this position would have been much more likely to hit the mark.

(7) When Lieutenant-Colonel P. A. Finch, an army doctor, was examining the dead President's body he found that one bullet had penetrated through the President's skin but had never come out and this is corroborated by an F.B.I. statement which reads: 'Medical examination of the President's body revealed that the bullet entered his back and penetrated to a distance of less than a finger length.' If this is true, and we must surely accept it, then the whole one-bullet theory of the Warren Commission falls to the ground, for the bullet could not possibly have hit Governor Connally who was sitting in front of the President and on a slightly lower level as well.

(8) The whole question of the bullets that killed the President could have been clarified by proper X-ray photographs which, of course, could have been interpreted by experts, but what the Commission was presented with were some medical drawings which may or may not have been accurate. Obviously this was highly unsatisfactory and one would have imagined that had the Commission been strong enough and ruthless enough they would have probed this matter to the hilt.

(9) The Commission did have available the evidence of three F.B.I. weapons experts and three army gunners with master ratings. These men attempted to achieve what Oswald was said to have done in fairly similar conditions although with a slightly better telescopic sight than Oswald was alleged to have used. Not one of them scored a hit on the head or neck of the dummy, so that we may think that it is asking too much to expect the public to believe that

Oswald, or any one else firing from the depository building window at a very considerable distance away, could have scored a shot which alone would have been certain to cause the President's death.

(10) The case for reopening the whole enquiry has been very much strengthened by the almost incredible death rate, since the murder, among those who would be valuable and perhaps essential witnesses.

Oswald, of course, was very quickly disposed of by Ruby, the owner of a somewhat sleazy night-club who appears to have been on remarkably intimate terms with the Dallas police whose duty and whose job it was to keep Oswald alive until he could be tried. Again there does not seem to have been any real probe into Ruby's motive. He was certainly not a man of high principle, outraged by a dastardly murder, and prepared to risk his life in a vengeful killing of the murderer. One thing is certain, that had Oswald faced trial he would have spoken. Now he can never speak and he was murdered in a manner which reflects gravely on the efficiency of the Dallas police who had him in custody.

Tom Howard, one of Ruby's lawyers, died of a heart attack in March 1965.

William Hunter, a Californian reporter, who was most tenacious in attempting to get at the truth, died as a result of a shooting accident in a police station in California in 1964.

Mr. James Koethe, a reporter of the *Dallas Times Herald*, who likewise was pursuing certain evidence he had unearthed, was quietly murdered in September 1964 by a murderer who it appears was an expert in karate.

A Mr. Killam, who was reliably said to know of a link between Oswald and Ruby, met a sudden accidental death in Florida some three years ago.

Lee Bowers, who was one of the witnesses who swore that the shooting came not from the deposi-

tory at all but from the high grassland by the road-
way, died in a car crash in Texas in August 1966.

Jane Mooney, who worked as a stripper in Jack
Ruby's Carousel Club, was unwise enough to have
given evidence that cleared a man who had been
charged with shooting a witness of the Warren
Commission. Miss Mooney was found hanged in a
Dallas police cell in 1964.

No wonder that the demand for a new and powerful
enquiry into the murder of President Kennedy grows.
The facts as we know them cast the gravest doubt
on the validity of the findings of the Warren Commission.
The world will not be happy and perhaps the United
States herself will not be content until another attempt,
far more ruthless than the first, has been made to unearth
the truth.

On that brilliant day in November in the city of Dallas
great evil had been done and a cold and objective review
of the facts so far revealed demand a fresh investigation
of an assassination that shook the world.

5

The Glories He Displayed

IN the autumn of 1965 I was invited to go to the T.W.W. television studios in Bristol to give an interview on my biography of Lord Butler. While we waited for our turn I chatted to a tall, spare man whose attitude and conversation seemed to reflect a certain disillusionment with life. He introduced himself as the present Lord Bath. Casting around for something to say to the owner of Longleat, I happened to mention that the previous week I had visited the Duke of Bedford, whose portrait I wanted to include in a proposed book on *English Worthies*. The Duke, I said, had had a wonderful year at Woburn and seemed to be leading the league in the public admission stakes.

I do not think the remark was a very tactful one. It was with particular relish that I read a paragraph recently in the gossip column of 'William Hickey' of the *Daily Express*, who comments so entertainingly on the activities of the great and famous. This is what I read:

'Lord Christopher Thynne, thirty-two-year-old photographer son of the Marquis of Bath, is worried about the way his career is going. He is now in demand to photograph buildings rather than people—which he prefers.

'People or things? His dilemma will not be improved on Tuesday night when his father leads a ghost hunt at their historic home, Longleat, Wilts.

'Lord Bath has organised a hunt for a relation of his named Lady Loise Cartaret, who has been dead for the past four hundred years. She is said to haunt Longleat. What sort of photograph would she make for Lord Christopher? I suspect his camera would show more architectural studies. Ghosts are difficult people to photograph.'

The Thynne family have been around since the reign of King John, when the first of them came over from Poitou in command of troops to assist the King in his war with the barons. They acquired great estates through the patronage of the Crown and by marriage so that in 1680, Sir James Thynne having died without issue, we find Thomas Thynne, Esq., of Longleat in Wiltshire, the overlord of a vast estate that included several villages and gave him an immense income. In order that we may savour the flavour of the Jacobean times we are moving in I quote from a report of this matter published in 1849.

'From his large income, Thomas Thynne was called Tom of Ten Thousand, and the society in which he moved was the highest in the land. He had been at one time a friend of the Duke of York, afterwards James II; but having quarrelled with His Royal Highness, he had latterly attached himself with great zeal to the Whig or opposition party in politics, and had become an intimate associate of their idol, or tool for the moment, the Duke of Monmouth. He had sate as one of the members for Wiltshire in four parliaments; and, after the prorogation to prevent the passing of the first Exclusion Bill, in July, 1679, he was one of the persons who went up to the King with a petition for the speedy recall of the great council of the nation; on which occasion his Majesty, addressing himself especially to Thynne, said he was amazed that persons of their estates should animate people to mutiny and rebellion, and that he wished they would mind their own affairs, and leave him to attend to his. At Longleat, where he lived in a style of great magnificence, Thynne was often visited by Monmouth; he is the Issachar of Dryden's glowing description, in the Absalom and Achitophel, of the Duke's popularity-and-plaudit gathering progresses:

From east to west his glories he displays,
And, like the sun, the Promised Land surveys.
Fame runs before him, as the morning star,
And shouts of joy salute him from afar;
Each house receives him as a guardian god,
And consecrates the place of his abode.
But hospitable treats did most commend
Wise Issachar, his wealthy western friend.

'A set of Oldenburgh coach-horses, of great beauty, which graced the Duke's equipage, had been presented to him by Thynne.

'The heiress of the house of Percy was nearly connected by affinity with families both of Lord Russell and Lord Cavendish; Lady Russell was a sister of her mother; and the family of her late husband, Lord Ogle, was a branch of that of the Earl of Devonshire; so that it may be supposed Thynne was probably in part indebted for his success in his suit to the good offices of his two noble friends. It should appear, however, from an entry in Evelyn's Diary, that the Duke of Monmouth was more instrumental than either.

'The lady was fated to be a second time wedded only in form; her marriage with Thynne appears to have taken place in the summer or autumn of this year, 1681; and she was separated from him immediately after the ceremony. One account is, that she fled from him of her own accord into Holland; another, and more probable version of the story, makes Thynne to have consented, at her mother's request, that she should spend a year on the Continent. It is to be remembered that she was not yet quite fifteen. The legality of the marriage, indeed, appears to have been called in question.

'It is now, as some say, that she first met Count Konigsmark at the Court of Hanover; but in this notion there is a confusion both of dates and persons. The Count, in fact, appears to have seen her in England, and to have paid his addresses to her before she gave her hand, or had it given for her, to Thynne: on his rejection he left the country; but that they met on the Continent there is no evidence or likelihood.

'Charles John Von Konigsmark was a Swede by birth, but was sprung from a German family, long settled in the district called the Mark of Brandenburg, on the coast of the Baltic. The name of Konigsmark is one of the most distinguished in the military annals of Sweden through a great part of the seventeenth century.'

So that now Thomas Thynne of Longleat has become involved in a great political matter as well as in a matrimonial situation. Perhaps it is necessary to say that at this time, and well into the nineteenth century, great heiresses were married for their money blatantly and without any real pretence that romance had entered into the matter. If the man had no fortune himself, society immediately called him a fortune-hunter and angry fathers were always willing, if they could catch the rascal, to thrash him within an inch—or two—of his life. But if the suitor was himself a man of great wealth then his alliance to a woman with a large fortune was regarded in an entirely different light. The system of *primo geniture* in England made it necessary, or at least advisable, for the heir to great estates to consolidate his position. Although he was not faced with death duties as he is at present, he was expected to maintain his brothers and sisters and their children, as well as his own, in suitable grandeur, and, to do him justice, he almost invariably did so. So an alliance with an heiress was entirely acceptable in such cases, approved by society, and greeted, of course, with suitable manifestations of ecstasy by those who lived as tenants or workmen on the estates concerned.

No one thought, at this time, that the affairs of Thomas Thynne would lead to trouble, far less to assassination and murder, but the situation had in it the elements of rivalry and intrigue, of great stakes and of high passion which may indeed lead to brutal and ruthless killing.

Let us follow the fortunes of John Von Konigsmark for

a little time. John was the head of his family and, like other continental aristocrats, he visited England from time to time. There was a belief among the nobility of the Continent that the fog in England occasionally lifted for a few weeks in June and July and John Von Konigsmark paid his first visit to England in the summer of 1674. He moved at once into the highest circles, for he had introductions from Paris, where his uncle, Count Otto William, had ensured his reception at court. But indeed John was so distinguished and accomplished a figure that he would probably have been acceptable without introductions. Three years later we find him in Italy and from Italy he goes to Malta to join the knights who were having much trouble with the Ottoman Empire to whom the existence of a Christian kingdom on Malta was a deadly provocation.

John set out on a cruise with the knights and, of course, displayed great courage and daring in an engagement with a Turkish vessel. He led the assault aboard the enemy craft and having ventured too far too soon was thrown into the waves and narrowly escaped being drowned because a Turk, without any chivalry at all, shot him through the foot with an arrow as he struggled in the sea. However, John Von Konigsmark was unsinkable and later we hear of him in Rome, Venice and Genoa, showing equal talents on the field of battle and in the boudoir. After visiting the courts of Portugal and Spain, where he managed to match the grandeur of the local grandees, he turned up again in England in the late spring of 1681.

At this time Tom of Ten Thousand, with the heiress of Northumberland his own by legal title, if not in actual possession, was at the height both of his personal and political fortunes. The idol of the patriotic enthusiasm of the day, his friend Monmouth, seemed already to have aspired to a throne; the absurd Popish plot and the murder of Sir Edmondbury Godfrey had done their work and raised a tempest which was so strong that the court had difficulty either in smothering it or in surviving against it.

Parliament after Parliament had been assembled at Westminster and at Oxford and after a few weeks dismissed with nothing accomplished. The Duke of York had taken refuge in Scotland. Lord Shaftesbury, the brains of the triumphant popular party, of which Monmouth was the ornamental headpiece, after having been detained for five months in the Tower on a charge of high treason had his indictment thrown out by the Grand Jury at the Old Bailey. He was restored to his freedom amidst immense public rejoicing. All London was illuminated that night with bonfires in his honour. England was alight with pending revolution. It was a background against which dreadful deeds might be done.

On the night of Sunday, 12th February 1682, King Charles at Whitehall heard the startling news that Thynne had been mortally shot passing along the public streets in his coach. The spot was towards the eastern extremity of Pall Mall, directly opposite to St. Albans Street, which no longer exists. A murder of such magnitude in the very heart of London created at first a stunned silence which exploded into a wild sensation. King Charles at Whitehall had been almost near enough to hear the report of the assassin's blunderbus, while Dryden, sitting in his favourite front room on the ground floor of his house on the south side of Gerald Street, was but two furlongs away.

Sir Jown Reresby, who himself took an active part in chasing and arresting the murderers, has left us a most graphic account of what happened as soon as the shots had been fired.

'This unhappy gentleman [Mr. Thynne] being much engaged in the Duke of Monmouth's cause, it was feared that party might put some violent construction on this accident, the actors therein making their escape just for the time, and being unknown. I happened to be at court that evening, when the King, hearing the news seemed greatly concerned at it, not only for the horror of the action itself (which was shocking to his natural disposition), but also for fear the turn the anti-court party might give thereto. I left the court, and was just stepping into bed when Mr. Thynne's gentleman came to me to grant him an Hue and Cry, and immediately at his heels comes the Duke of Monmouth's page, to desire me to come to him at Mr. Thynne's lodging, sending his coach for me, which I made use of accordingly. I there found his grace surrounded with several lords and gentlemen, Mr. Thynne's friends, and Mr. Thynne himself mortally wounded with five shots from a blunderbuss. I, on the spot, granted several warrants against persons supposed to have had a hand therein, and that night got some intelligence concerning the actors themselves. At length, by the information of a chairman, who had carried one of the ruffians from his lodging at Westminster to the Black Bull, there to take horse, and by means of a woman, who used to visit the same person, the constable found out the place of his abode, and there took his man, by nation a Swede, who, being brought before me, confessed himself a servant to a German Captain, who had told him he had a quarrel with Mr. Thynne, and had often ordered him to watch his coach; and that particularly that day the Captain no sooner understood the coach to be gone by than he booted himself, and, with two others, a Swedish Lieutenant and a Pole, went on horseback, as he supposed in quest of Mr. Thynne. By the same servant I also understood where possibly the Captain and his two companions were to be found; and having, with the Duke of Monmouth, Lord Mordaunt, and others, searched several houses, as he directed us, till six in the morning, and having been in close pursuit all night, I personally took the Captain in the house of a Swedish doctor in Leicester Fields.'

On Friday the 17th two men were arrested, the first was a Pole named Borosky and the second a Swedish lieutenant named Stern. They were both examined before Sir John Reresby and William Bridgman, who was another Middlesex magistrate. Magisterial examinations were more inquisitorial at this time and the rules of legal procedure which have been built up to protect the accused were not operating, or, in so far as they were, they were frequently ignored. Both men confessed that they had taken part in the assassination. Borosky said that he had come to England at the request of Count Konigsmark, having been recruited by an agent of the Count in Hamburg. He did not know what he would have to do in England, but on a Saturday some weeks previous to the assassination the Count told him that he had had a quarrel with an English gentleman who had set six persons upon him while he was travelling upon the road, but two of the assailants were killed. The Count went on to say that as Mr. Thynne had attempted to kill him, he would make an end of it. Borosky then told the magistrates that the Count had said: 'Tomorrow will come a certain servant to conduct you to the Captain, and what he bids you to do, that you are to observe.' According to Borosky, a man did come on Sunday morning at about eleven o'clock and took him to another house where he found the person who conveyed him to the Captain who gave him a musquetoon and a pocket pistol as well as a sword. The Captain said to Borosky, repeating it several times slowly: 'When we go out together if I stop a coach do you fire into it and then follow me:' So they took horse and met the coach and the Captain cried 'Hold!' The Captain ordered Borosky to fire and he did fire and the murder was done.

Thynne had survived his mortal wounds only a few hours during which the Duke of Monmouth sat by the bedside of his dying friend. He died at six in the morning. A search for Count Konigsmark was successful and he and three other prisoners, after being examined, were lodged in Newgate and, an indictment having been made against them by the Grand Jury, they were the next day brought up to the bar at the Old Bailey to be arraigned and tried—Charles George Borosky, Christopher Vratz and John Stern as principals in the murder and Charles John, Count Konigsmark, as accessary before the fact. The trial began at nine o'clock in the morning.

The evidence was clear that Borosky had shot Thynne and that Vratz and Stern had assisted him. The evidence against Count Konigsmark was less direct, but one would have thought might easily have led to his conviction. It was proved that he had taken a room in a very poor lodging and had held communication with the murderers. There was also some evidence of his anger against Thynne for espousing Lady Ogle. His defence was that the accused men, being his servants, he had of necessity much communication with them, but he knew nothing of the murder nor had he had any quarrel with Mr. Thynne.

Count Konigsmark was extremely lucky. He was acquitted when one would have thought he would have been found guilty as an accessary before the fact. His acquittal may have been due in part to the rule of evidence that insisted that the evidence of accomplices shall not be held as valid against an accessary before the fact, but in this case the Count probably owed his life to Chief Justice Pemberton, who presided over, and indeed dominated, the trial. The summing-up of the Chief Justice is a document both artful and cunning. It was patently favourable to the Count. The Chief Justice, according to those who attended the trial, seemed quite determined to save Konigsmark. Is it possible that the Establishment was not ready to see Konigsmark suffer for the murder of Thynne, who was the rebel Duke of Monmouth's great ally and friend?

There is a tomb of white marble for Thomas Thynne at the west end of the south aisle of Westminster Abbey. His effigy shows him in his coach, with three assassins, one stopping the horse, the second securing the footmen behind, whilst the third shoots him, The tomb was made at the cost of his executor and brother-in-law John Hall and a eulogistic inscription in Latin was prepared and it was intended that this should be engraved upon it, but Dr. Thomas Spratt, the Bishop of Rochester, who was also Dean of Westminster, refused to allow the inscription which he thought might not find favour with the government, which, of course, included court circles. So the tomb to this day bears the simple inscription:

'Thomas Thynne, of Longleate, in the county of Wilts, Esquire, who was barbarously murdered on Sunday, 12th February, 1682.'

Count Konigsmark left England as fast as he could, having paid his fees and got out of the hands of the officers of justice at the Old Bailey.

Oh, yes, and I almost forgot to mention that the convicted prisoners were hanged in Pall Mall, to the public satisfaction, on the 10th of March the following year. The infamous Borosky, who fired the blunderbuss, was suspended in chains near Mile End until he rotted. Thus the nice class distinctions of the seventeenth century were maintained and everyone was, more or less, happy.

6

A Madness Indiscreet

I AM one of those people who find it difficult to go up to complete strangers at receptions and talk to them glibly, as one should do, on the assumption, unwritten but valid, that all the guests because they have been invited by the same host know each other 'constructively', as the lawyers would say.

I therefore was relieved when I entered a large room full of people, most of whom I had never seen before, in London recently to see the imposing almost magisterial figure of Victor Montagu standing head and shoulders above most of the guests. If he made those immediately surrounding him look a little like serfs that was not his fault. His ruddy complexion, blue eyes, handsome visage and fine physique, not to mention the efforts of his excellent tailor, give one the impression of an Englishman who has just stepped, albeit reluctantly, out of the late seventeenth or early eighteenth century. This is a happy coincidence, for the assassination of Miss Reay, the story I am about to tell, very much concerned the Fourth Lord Sandwich, John Montagu.

I talked to Victor Montagu for a few minutes and he told me that he was thinking of writing a book, not an autobiography but a book of political reminiscence and comment. We discussed how he should set about this. My advice to him was first to contact a prestige publisher and secondly to be sure that he was paid money as an advance against royalties, because this would show that the publisher was seriously interested. I suggested he should contact Lord Hardinge of Penhurst, with whom I had had some correspondence, because I thought the two peers might get on together and I was not so sure that Victor Montagu would find some publishers in the new highly competitive book world congenial. He took my advice and then sat down and wrote me a letter saying he was grateful. He had inherited the title of Earl of Sandwich but, of course, it was as Viscount Hinchingbrooke that he had played a leading part generally on the right wing of the Tory party for many years. I only recalled this incident when I came across the terrible assassination of Miss Reay by the Rev. Mr. Hackman.

Miss Reay was the daughter of a stay-maker in Covent Garden and served her apprenticeship to a mantua-maker in George's Court, St. John's Lane, Clerkenwell. She was bound when only thirteen and during her apprenticeship was noticed by Lord Sandwich who took her under his protection and treated her with every mark of tenderness. At the time of being introduced to Mr. Hackman she had lived with her noble protector during a period of nineteen years, and in the course of that time had borne nine children. One of the children by this union became an eminent member of the English Bar. Although Miss Reay was nearly twice the age of Mr. Hackman, no sooner had he seen her than he became violently enamoured of her.

James Hackman was born in Gosport in Hampshire and, in the words of a contemporary chronicler, was 'originally designed for trade, in which his father was engaged'. It was found, however, that he was too volatile by nature to have any success in business and his parents, who were not poor, purchased for him a commission as an ensign in the 68th Regiment of Foot. He had not been in the service very long when he was entrusted with the command of a recruiting party and going to Huntingdon, under orders, he became known to the Earl of Sandwich whose seat was nearby. The Earl, who liked the young man, asked him to dinner on several occasions. In this way he first became acquainted with the object of his passion and the victim of his fury.

A Corporal Trim acted as letter bearer between the ardent ensign and the object of his affections.

Shortly after arriving in Huntingdon he was already writing daily to Miss Reay and it is clear that he was asking Margaret Reay to leave Lord Sandwich, to whom, of course, she was not married, and to come away with him. James Hackman had a certain literary gift which might be over-ornate but somehow conveyed an absolute sincerity. They must have been shattering letters for a middle-aged woman to receive. For instance, on the 6th December 1775, writing from Huntingdon, he penned this remarkable explosion of devotion which shows both his literary style and, I think, the peculiar urgency of his feelings:

'My dearest Margaret, No, I will not take advantage of the sweet, reluctant, amorous confession which your candour gave me yesterday. If to make me happy be to make my M. otherwise, then, happiness, I'll none of thee.

'And yet I *could* argue. Suppose he *has* bred you up— suppose you *do* owe your numerous accomplishments, under genius to him—are you therefore his property? Is it as if a horse that he has bred up should refuse to carry him? Suppose you therefore *are* his property will the fidelity of so many years weigh nothing in the scale of gratitude?

'Years! why, can obligation (suppose they had *not* been repaid an hundredfold) do away the unnatural disparity of years? Can they bid five-and-fifty stand still (the least that you could ask), and wait for five-and-twenty? Many women have the same obligations (if, indeed, there be many of the *same* accomplishments) to their fathers. They have the additional obligation to them (if indeed, it be an obligation) of existence. The disparity of years is sometimes even less. But, must they therefore take their fathers to their bosoms? Must the jessamine fling its tender arms around the dying elm?

'To my little fortunes you are no stranger. Will you share them with me? And you shall honestly tell his Lordship that gratitude taught you to pay every duty to him till love taught you there were other duties which you owed to H.

'Gracious Heaven, that you would pay them!

'But, did I not say I would not take advantage? I will not. I will even remind you of your children; to whom I, alas! could only shew at present the affection of a father.

'M., weigh us in the scales. If gratitude out-balance love —so.

'If you command it, I swear by love, I'll join my regiment tomorrow.

'If love prevail, and insist upon his dues, you shall declare the victory and the prize. I *will* take no advantage.

'Think over this. Neither will I take you by surprise. *Sleep upon it*, before you return your answer. Trim shall make the old excuse tomorrow. And, thank Heaven, tonight you sleep alone!

'Why did you sing that sweet song yesterday, though I so pressed you? Those words and your voice were too much.

'No word can say how much I am yours.'

James Hackman, who does not seem to have been a young man who had really decided what he wanted to do in life, thought that his chances of preferment in the army were not as good as he had hoped. He then turned his thoughts towards the Church and took Holy Orders. He had not to wait long for the living of Wiverton in Norfolk. He moved into the vicarage there just before Christmas in 1778. By this time his passion for Margaret Reay had become almost uncontrollable. Margaret Reay had made it quite clear that she was not going to desert Lord Sandwich and, though flattered by the extraordinary devotion of so young a man, James Hackman was forced to face the end of the affair, if one can call it that. He wrote to his friend Charles Ritchie on the 6th of April 1779 and the letter clearly shows that he had become demented about this matter. Had the letter been produced before a modern court which might have been convinced of the young man's genuineness there is no doubt that a defence of diminished responsibility at the trial of Hackman for the murder of Miss Reay would have had some chance of success. But this was still the eighteenth century and the penalty for murder was the crack of the rope and no excuses. The letter to Ritchie shows so clearly the instability of his mind that I risk boring the reader by quoting it in full.

'It signifies not. Your reasoning I admit. Despair goads me on. Death only can relieve me. By what I wrote yesterday, you must see my resolution was taken. Often have I made use of my key to let myself into the A., that I might die at her feet. She gave it me as the key of love—Little did she think it would ever prove the key of death. But the loss of Lady H. keeps Lord S. within.

'My dear Charles, is it possible for me to doubt G.'s information? Even you were staggered by the account I gave you of what passed between us in the Park. What then have I to do, who only lived when she loved me, but to cease to live now she ceased to love? The propriety of suicide, its cowardice, its crime—I have nothing to do with them. All I pretend to prove or disprove is my misery, and the possibility of my existing under it. Enclosed are the last dying words and confession of poor Captain J,. who destroyed himself not long ago. But these lines are not the things which have determined me. There are many defects in the reasoning of them, though none in the poetry. His motives are not mine, nor are his principles mine. *His* ills I could have borne. He told me of his inducements, poor fellow! But I refused to allow them. Little did I imagine that I should ever have inducements, as I now have, which I *must* allow. These extra-ordinary lines are said to be his. Yet, from what I knew of him, I am slow to believe it. They strike me as the production of abilities far superior to his; of abilities sent into the world for some particular purpose, and which Providence would not suffer to quit the world in such a manner.

'Till within this month, till G.'s information, I thought of self-murder as you think of it. Nothing now is left for me but to leap the world to come. If it be a crime, as I too much fear, and we are accountable for our passions. I must stand the trials and the punishment. My invention can point to punishment equal to what I suffer here.

'Think of those passions, my friend—those passions of which you have so often, since I knew Miss ——, spoken to me and written to me. If you will not let me fly from my misery, will you not let me fly from my passions? They are a pack of bloodhounds which will inevitably tear me to pieces. My carelessness has suffered them to overtake me, and now there is no possibility but this, of escaping them. The hand of Nature heaped up every species of combustible in my bosom. The torch of love has set the heap on fire. I must perish in the flames. At first I might perhaps have extinguished them—now they rage too fiercely. *If* they can be smothered, they can never be got under. Suppose they should consume any other person beside myself. And who is he will answer for passions such as mine?—At present, I am innocent.'

Between the two letters I have quoted over a period of nearly three years James Hackman wrote a series of love-letters to Margaret Reay which even today have an extraordinary force and freshness. For instance, on the 7th December 1775 he wrote to her:

'My dearest Soul, I hope to heaven Trim will be able to get this to you tonight! Not I only, but my whole future life, shall thank you for the dear sheet of paper I have just received. Blessings! Blessings! But I could write and exclaim and offer up vows and prayers till the happy hour arrives!'

It is clear, I think, that at this stage Margaret Reay had not the courage, nor perhaps the inclination, to cut the young man off. It was a situation over which the black cloud of tragedy loomed from the start. On the morning of the 7th April 1779 Hackman had lodged in Duke's Court, St. Martin's Lane. There he sat for some time in his closet reading *Blair's Sermons*, but in the evening he took a walk to the Admiralty, where he saw Miss Reay go into the coach with Señora Galli, who attended her. The coach drove to Covent Garden Theatre, where the ladies stayed to see the performance of *Love in a Village*. James Hackman went into the theatre at that time, but he soon returned to his lodging. He loaded two pistols, returning to the playhouse, where he waited till the play was over.

Seeing Miss Reay ready to step into the coach, he took a pistol in each hand, one of which he discharged against her. She died on the spot. The other pistol he discharged against himself, but it did not take effect. He then beat himself with the butt end on his head in order to destroy himself, but after a struggle he was secured, his wounds were dressed and he was carried before Sir John Fielding, who committed him to Newgate. On the direction of Sir John he was not allowed to be alone for fear he should commit suicide.

On the day of the murder he had dined with his sister and in the afternoon he wrote a letter to her husband, Mr. Booth, an eminent attorney, saying that he intended to destroy himself and asking him to sell whatever property he left and pay a small debt which he owed. The letter was never sent. It was found in his pocket. But, of course, the writing of the letter might be said to indicate a premeditated crime, though Miss Reay was not mentioned in the letter.

The prisoner was indicted at the next sessions at the Old Bailey and tried before Mr. Justice Backstone, the author of the famous *commentaries* and perhaps the most distinguished British lawyer of the eighteenth century.

There was one curious incident proved at the trial and that was that a Mr. MacNamara, who knew Miss Reay slightly as an acquaintance, was leaving the theatre at the

same time as Miss Reay and her companion and offered
her his arm to step up into her coach. At this moment the
shot was fired. It could, of course, have been that to the
demented Hackman the gesture had a significance of in-
timacy which it would not have conveyed to anyone else.
James Hackman made a statement which was, in effect, a
confession. But he also made it quite clear that he had
acted while subject to an uncontrollable, or at least un-
controlled, passion. And it was also not seriously disputed
that he had made a desperate effort to take his own life.
Of course, from the point of view of the lawyers at this
time, this was not a mitigating circumstance. Self-murder,
or attempted self-murder, was no excuse for the murder
of another being. It has taken nearly two hundred years
for the legal conception of suicide as self-murder to be
challenged and even today it is only a matter of debate,
the law remains as adamant as ever. James Hackman was
very conscious that the crime he had committed had
been committed by him when he was a priest and his
despair and shame came out clearly in the statement he
made to the judge.

'I should not have troubled the court with the examination of witnesses to support the charge against me, had I
not thought that the pleading guilty to the indictment gave
an indication of contemning death, not suitable to my
present condition, and was, in some measure, being acces-
sory to a second peril of my life: and I therefore thought
that the justice of my country ought to be satisfied by
suffering my offence to be proved, and the fact established
by evidence.

'I stand here this day the most wretched of human
beings, and confess myself criminal in a high degree; yet
while I acknowledge, with shame and repentence, that my
determination against my own life was formal and complete, I protest, with that regard to truth which becomes
my situation, that the will to destroy her, who was ever
dearer to me than life, was never mine till a momentary
frenzy overcame me, and induced me to commit the deed

I now deplore. The letter which I meant for my brother-in-law after my decease will have its due weight as to this point with good men.

'Before this dreadful act I trust nothing will be found in the tenor of my life, which the common charity of mankind will not excuse. I have no wish to avoid the punishment which the laws of my country appoint for my crime; but being already too unhappy to feel a punishment in death or a satisfaction in life, I submit myself with penitence and impatience to the disposal and judgment of Almighty God, and to the consequences of this inquiry into my conduct and intention.'

Mr. Justice Blackstone put on the black cap and spoke the dreadful words of the death sentence after the jury had returned their verdict of guilty. James Hackman, now absolutely calm, seemed resigned to his fate. He employed the very short time then allowed murderers after conviction in writing letters and in repentence and prayer.

The awful ritual procession to Tyburn took place. The convicted man was removed from his coach to the cart and the rope was put round his neck. As this was done he took leave of Dr. Porter and the Ordinary in an affectionate manner and crossed himself. The great crowd which had collected to witness the execution remained curiously silent without the drunkenness and cat-calling which was common at public executions at this time. Something about the man's demeanour and perhaps the fact that he was dying a priest stilled the crowd.

At a word of command the cart was driven away and James Hackman was hanging there, just after three o'clock on a beautiful spring day, the 19th April 1779.

James Hackman died almost immediately. It was not necessary for the two executioners to strangle him by pulling on his legs, as so often happened at this time. The law had exacted its penalty. The crowd was already dispersing. Perhaps they had come to see the usual dramatic entertainment, but they went away quietly, as if conscious that they had seen the last act in a great tragedy.

7

Stage-managed

ABRAHAM LINCOLN, President of the United States during the most momentous period of its history, was the
grandson of Abraham Lincoln who had been killed by
Indians in 1784 and the son of Thomas Lincoln of Vir-
ginia by his wife Nancy Hanks. He was born on the 12th
February 1809 in Harden, Kentucky.

The family moved to Spencer County, Indiana, building the log hut in which they lived. A Mr. Crawford came
to settle in the neighbourhood and opened a school for
the local children in his own cabin. Abraham attended
this school and must have been something of a trial to his
more unruly schoolmates, for by common consent he had
an absolute thirst for knowledge, was unnaturally earnest
for a boy of his age and almost painfully truthful. The
books that he loved and read did not include the wild
adventure stories which were then beginning to circulate.
He preferred Bunyan's *Pilgrim's Progress*, Aesop's
Fables, a life of Henry Clay, and a life of Washington. At a
very early age he knew the American story from the beginning and this knowledge was to stand him in good stead in
his future life.

When he was nineteen Abraham made a trip to New
Orleans in a flat boat, with the son of one of his neighbours, and with a cargo for the New Orleans market.
In addition to a long voyage down the River Ohio, the
two young men had at least a thousand miles of the Missis-

sippi to travel before they arrived at their journey's end. The success of this enterprise raised the standing of Abraham Lincoln in the eyes of his neighbours, but he was still very young and had not found his true vocation.

About two years after this in 1830, when Abraham was twenty-one, he migrated with his father to Decatur, Illinois. Again he helped to build the family log hut, and he also found employment as a 'rail-splitter', performing the remarkable feat of splitting about three thousand rails a day. Abraham hired himself out as a labourer and sometimes as a clerk or book-keeper. In 1832 war broke out with the Indians, the war that was called at the time the Black Hawk War. Abraham was appointed to command a company of volunteers and he served with some distinction. His war service increased his authority and cemented his already formidable character, so that he was able, when he returned to civilian life, to keep a store and later to set up in business as a surveyor. In 1834 he was sent to the local legislature and during the time the house was not sitting he applied himself to the study of law with his usual determined dedication. He received a licence to practise in 1836 and next year went into partnership with the Honourable John F. Stewart, conducting a rapidly increasing legal practice. He was very successful as an advocate in jury trials. In 1846 he was returned to Congress and took his seat as the only Whig member from Illinois. The Whigs were the forerunners of the present Republican Party.

So that at the age of forty we find Abraham Lincoln, who was generally admitted to be both a good and a great man, on the verge of a national career in the young and rapidly expanding United States. There is no room in this chapter to trace the whole of his political career, but one fact stands out and runs like a golden thread through the whole of his story. He was opposed to slavery and himself calculated that he had cast his vote in favour of freeedom on this issue no less than forty-six times. He opposed the Mexican war, for curiously enough, slavery was illegal under Mexican law many years before it became illegal under United States law.

In 1849 Abraham stood for the office of United States Senator for Illinois. He was defeated, so for a time he returned to the practise of his profession. Lincoln's opponent in Illinois was Stephen A. Douglas and the two champions, in the best democratic tradition, held seven debates in different towns of the state with a view to showing the people why they differed on the crucial question of slavery. As sometimes happens when confrontation is indulged in by politicians, the meetings and debates between Lincoln and Douglas attracted the attention of the whole United States. The immediate question was, during the presidential election of 1860, whether slavery ought to be permitted in the new territories as one by one they were included in the Union. Lincoln believed that slavery ought to be excluded from these territories, although he had not yet reached the point when he could bring himself to exclude slavery from territories in which it was already established.

It is never quite possible to say what it is that attracts a public to the oratory or rhetoric of one man. We can only quote examples of this. Lord Randolph Churchill, even when he held no official position, could always command the attention of the English people and the same, of course, applied to his son. Perhaps it was their mixture of honesty, daring, deep sincerity, truculence and mischief, coupled with a great mastery of words in combat, that made this possible. The same perhaps applied to Abraham Lincoln. Of course, the orator must have his cause and that cause must be a sufficiently burning issue to compel attention in its own account. At this time slavery or antislavery was such an issue and Abraham Lincoln was such an orator. Underlying the public debates on immediate legislation either to permit slavery or to make it illegal lay the question of what kind of a country the United States was going to be, and this involved the very critical question of internal race relations.

In 1860, when Abraham Lincoln was forty-nine, the Republican Convention met in Chicago and nominated Lincoln as their candidate for the presidency. Lincoln defeated Mr. Seward and, although the campaign was carried on with good humour from the North, in the South there were angry mutterings and threats. The poll was declared and Lincoln had polled one million, eight hundred and fifty-seven thousand, nine hundred and ten votes. The runner-up, Douglas, polled six hundred thousand votes less, and two other candidates, though polling substantially, were left a long way behind.

The election of Lincoln was hailed with frenzied delight by the people of the Northern states and when he travelled to Washington to take up the office of President the whole country watched his progress. He was installed in the President's chair on the 4th March 1861.

The election of Lincoln had, however, a terrible repercussion. It was followed by the secession of eleven Southern states and this led to the Civil War for the restoration of the Union. Lincoln's instinct was to woo the South, appealing for them to submit to authority and to return to legality. He failed in his appeal. On the 1st January 1863 Lincoln proclaimed the freedom of all slaves in the rebel states and afterwards the absolute freedom of the Negroes throughout the country. He was re-elected as President in 1865 and after conducting the war to a successful conclusion he had the satisfaction of establishing the authority of the Union over the whole country. This was, in brief, the career of one of the most remarkable men of recent history. In the story of America there is no one to compare to Lincoln except George Washington. His foul assassination on Good Friday, the 14th of April 1865, and his death on the following day, therefore created complete consternation not only in America but throughout the world.

The South had been defeated, but the burning hatred of war and the gall of defeat had bitten deeply into the Southern character. It was almost inevitable that from this huge resentment some character would be thrown up who determined on a deed, however reckless and dastardly, that would avenge the defeat of the South for all time. This was filled by John Wilkes Booth, an actor. Now the life of an actor consists very largely in portraying fiction as if it were fact and good actors are apt to become so immersed in their fictional role that they themselves are apt to assume in fact and in life the characteristics of their fictional personification. However this may be, I think it can be said that actors are not as other men are.

Booth identified himself with all the burning resentment of the South and he determined to play his last and by far his greatest role. He would assassinate Lincoln. And he would assassinate him in the most dramatic possible way at the theatre.

April the 14th, Good Friday, found the President with his wife in Washington with a free evening. They had decided to go to Ford's Theatre that night with General and Mrs. Grant. The Grants were unable to come and Mrs. Lincoln invited a Major Rathbone and his young fiancée, Miss Clara Harris, to go with them.

Rather late, the President and his wife got into their carriage, which was driven by Burns, their coachman, with Forbes, the President's valet, sitting next to him. Such was the simple way in which an American President then travelled. However, at the theatre, they were met by a detective called Parker, who belonged to the Washington City Police and whose duty it was to act as the President's bodyguard that evening. The President and his wife, followed by Major Rathbone and his fiancée, walked towards the President's box, which was gaily decorated. They were received by a terrific and spontaneous burst of applause, the whole audience standing, the leading lady, Laura Keene, stopping the play to join in the applause and the band playing 'Hail to the Chief'.

The President's two servants, as well as Parker the detective, were presumed to be in the vicinity of the presidential box, so that in fact three men were near the President's person when he first sat down, but from where they sat in the passage behind the presidential box they could not see the play and no doubt became bored with waiting so they all went off and had a drink in the bar. This was the moment that Booth had been waiting for. He knew the play very well and he knew that the whole action centred on an English grande dame, Mrs. Mount Chessington, who believed that her young American cousin was a millionaire when in fact he was penniless. It was the discovery by Mrs. Mount Chessington that all her plans had crashed that led to the apex of the play and a moment when the audience was wont to burst into a great round of applause prior to a curtain. At this moment all other noises in the theatre would be blotted out.

Booth was the most deliberate of assassins. He had gained entrance to the theatre that afternoon with the excuse that he would like to witness a rehearsal and he had tampered with the locks of the presidential box. He had also bored a hole in the partition to the rear of the presidential box through which, with one eye, he could see not only the President but his party as well, and, as it was in a larger focus, most of the theatre and the stage. Booth crept into the passage, looked through his peephole and saw that Laura Keene was leading up to the denouement of the play. The crisis line was spoken and, as expected, the audience burst into a deafening round of applause in which the presidential party joined. Booth very quietly opened the door of the box and shot the President at point-blank range through the head. Major Rathbone attempted to seize him but he broke loose and sprang from the box on to the stage. He injured a foot badly in doing this but in the pandemonium he managed to escape, for the time being, to his horse, which was waiting nearby. He rode out furiously into the night.

Back in the theatre at first no one realised what had happened. Mrs. Lincoln herself did not understand. Her husband's body showed no obvious sign of mutilation. Then someone raised the agonised cry: 'He has shot the

President', and the whole house suddenly became aware of the terrible tragedy that had been enacted in the Ford Theatre that night. A young doctor, Dr. Leele, rushed to the presidential box and attended the President. Dr. Leele saw that the President was too ill to return to his house. They took him to the house of a Mr. Peterson, a tailor, who lived next door to the theatre.

At twenty minutes past seven the following morning the President died. It is doubtful whether even modern techniques of blood transfusion could have saved him. The damage to his brain was too great. When it was realised that Lincoln was dead the Secretary of War, Stanton, said: 'Now he belongs to the ages.'

The assassination of Lincoln, in its time and day, was as horrible and as atrocious as the assassination of John Kennedy less than a century later.

Queen Victoria had lost her Albert not so long before this tragedy and the letter which she immediately wrote to Mrs. Lincoln from Osborne showed the grief of the widow of England for the widow of America and at the same time reflected the restraint and dignity with which such matters were then treated. This was the Queen's letter:

Osborne,
29th April, 1865.

Dear Madam,

Though a stranger to you I cannot remain silent when so terrible a calamity has fallen upon you and your country, and must express personally my deep and heartfelt sympathy with you under the shocking circumstances of your present dreadful misfortune. No one can better appreciate than I can, who am myself utterly broken-hearted by the loss of my own beloved husband who was the light of my life, my stay, my all, what your suffering must be; and I earnestly pray that you may be supported by Him to whom alone the sorely stricken can look for comfort in this hour of heavy affliction.

With the renewed expression of true sympathy I remain, dear Madam, your sincere friend.

Victoria R.

To this letter on the 21st May 1865 Mary Lincoln replied with equal dignity and compassion. This is what she wrote:

Madam,

I have received the letter which your Majesty has had the kindness to write, and am deeply grateful for its expressions of tender sympathy coming as they do, from a heart which from its own sorrow, can appreciate the *intense grief* I now endure.

Accept, Madam, the assurance of my heartfelt thanks and believe me in the deepest sorrow your Majesty's sincere and grateful friend.

Mary Lincoln

The two widows, Queen Victoria and Mary Lincoln, both seem to have been devoted to their husbands by quite exceptional ties of love and indeed of adoration. When death deprived them of the star that illuminated their lives, both of them were plunged into a grief so deep and so protracted that it became somewhat abnormal. The Queen in England, after the death of Prince Albert, practically went into hiding for over twenty years. For many years she insisted on wearing her widow's weeds and the death of Albert in one form or another was apt to colour all her conversation. This was particularly awkward for statesmen she disliked, such as Mr. Gladstone, because, when she was confronted with a situation which demanded her decision, but from which she wanted to escape, she could always cry out: 'If only my dear Albert was here to help me now!'

This does not mean that she was not genuine about the matter. She certainly was, but she went to extraordinary lengths to keep the memory of Albert alive in the royal household. His bedroom, together with all his clothes and personal belongings, was kept exactly as he had left it. The room was aired and dusted and polished and cleaned as carefully and as meticulously as if the Prince was still using it. This did not mean that the Queen was mentally deranged—she could be very astute when she wanted to be—but it did mean that the death of her husband made her an entirely different kind of person whose reactions to certain situations were unusual and unexpected if in some way they sparked off the memory of Albert.

Likewise with Mary Lincoln the death of her husband had a lasting effect on her approach to life. She became morbidly fearful least she should be left in penury without a room to shelter her. There was never, in fact, any danger of this, for her husband's estate, though modest for a President, was quite substantial and Congress quickly voted her an adequate annual grant. I find it interesting that two women so far apart in most matters should have this in common, that they grieved for their husbands more than it is usually possible for human nature to sustain.

Can we trace a common link in the assassination of Lincoln and Kennedy? Perhaps it could be so. Lincoln was the man who more than any other American set the slaves free. John Kennedy, it was thought, intended to do away with racial discrimination and pursue the ideal of a wholly integrated society.

8

Irish Revenge

THURSDAY, the 22nd of June 1922, was, of course, the height of the season in London, and it really seemed as if, in spite of the deadliest great war in history, nothing had really changed. Many of the great houses of London were still standing, though Devonshire House in Piccadilly had already been sold and it was said that vast office buildings, including motor-car sale-rooms, would be erected on the site.

The British Empire had come through the ordeal of war almost untouched, and indeed it had been extended by the appropriation of some former German colonies, either directly or under mandate from the League of Nations. The King of England was still Emperor of India and the Parliament at Westminster ruled approximately a quarter of the globe.

A traveller leaving London by ship for the Far East never had to call at a foreign port—Gibraltar, Malta, Suez and Port Said, Aden, Karachi, Bombay, Colombo, Port Sweetenham, Penang, Singapore, Hong Kong, they were all British or subject to a direct British influence. It was the greatest empire that the world had ever seen. Compared with it the Roman Empire was a provincial European affair with tendrils reaching out into Asia Minor and North Africa. The war that had ended in the defeat of Germany four years before had brought America out of isolation into the centre of world affairs, but it had not displaced Britain as one of the greatest nations of the world. The carnage of the war had been unbelievable. Under old-fashioned generals, of whom the most notable was Sir Douglas Haig, infantrymen had been sent to take positions which were protected by trenches, barbed wire and machine-guns. Almost a generation of young Englishmen had been wiped out.

The mood of the country was a reaction against the terrible and grim years that had passed. This was the beginning of the twenties. Now, for the first time since the Victorian age, well-established social and moral values were to be questioned. It was to be a decade of sexual liberation and, in London at any rate, of sexual freedom.

One complex and terrible situation had not been entirely resolved. This was the Irish question. The 1916 rebellion had been suppressed as it had to be, for England was at war and was not prepared to tolerate treachery anywhere, but after the war it became clear that the Protestant Irish of the North, largely of Scottish descent, were determined to have their own government, which would mean that when independence came to Ireland the six northern counties would be excluded from the settlement and would, in fact, have a government of their own.

No one wanted this division of Ireland, but the Ulstermen were adamant and, led by Carson and F. E. Smith, they were extremely articulate. They said that Ulster would fight, and to prove it they raised the Ulster Volunteers.

The civil war in Ireland had brought about indescribable bitterness on both sides. The Irish rebels could operate only as guerillas and to the occupying British forces the sudden ambushes and arsons that they brought about seemed to be cowardly murder. This led to retaliation and the Irish backed their Republican Army, believing that they were fighting despotism.

The Irish as a nation and as a people have a considerable capacity for hatred and do not forget and forgive readily. The people they hated most were the Irish, often of British descent, in the South who sided with the English. Henry Wilson was one of these. He was military adviser to the Belfast authorities and by nature a man who made many friends and innumerable enemies, for he was a disciplinarian, a military genius and had a tongue that could lash his enemies so that they never forgot. By 1922 he had left the army and entered the House of Commons. He lived at 36 Eaton Place with his wife Lady Wilson, and, as Field Marshal Sir Henry Wilson Bart., G.C.B., D.S.O., M.P., he was a legendary figure to the English public with a great record of service to England which had ended by his being Chief of the Imperial General Staff. In fact he really was not only distinguished but extremely able. Perhaps his greatest contribution to the defeat of Germany was his insistence that Allied forces in France should have one commander, and that commander should be Marshal Foch.

Although in June 1922 Wilson had left the Irish scene, the Irish had not forgotten him and they sentenced him to death, that is to say they decided to murder him in cold blood. We have the word of Joe Dolan that Michael Collins sent an order to execute Wilson to Sam Maguire, who was the chief spy of the Irish Republican Army in the London area. This was a terrible and evil plot. The Irish rebels knew very well that Sir Henry Wilson had carried out his duties in Ireland with scrupulous regard for the rules of war. He had protested against the importation of the Black and Tans. He was a soldier, a British soldier, and he hated indiscipline, feuding and private revenge. Nevertheless, for the Irish, Wilson typified the stern, relentless rule of the British, with their insufferable assumption of superiority, their conviction that they could rule other people better than other people could rule themselves.

On the 22nd of June Sir Henry Wilson had dedicated a memorial to those who had fallen in the war. Patriotism was not yet a dirty word and at the end of his speech he was able to quote to a hushed and responsive audience Kipling's words beginning: 'The tumult and the shouting dies; ...'

Sir Henry returned by taxi to his house in Eaton Place, calling for a moment at the Travellers' Club in Pall Mall on the way. There was some traffic congestion and the journey took longer than it should have done. However, at last, the taxi drew up in front of the house. Sir Henry got out and started to pay the taxi man and then turned to open his door. The inevitable road-repair gang who were working on a pavement took no notice of two men who had been lurking in the square for half an hour and who, some minutes before, had so stationed themselves that they commanded a clear and close view of the few yards between the taxi and the door. They shot him in the back, with typical Irish chivalry, four times. He fell heavily and crashed into the gutter. Lady Wilson rushed out. Her husband was dying. The square, which had been decorous and almost drowsy a moment before, erupted into a scene of incredible confusion and anger. The two murderers fled, jumping into a victoria. They threatened to murder the driver, so he drove them off at speed, but they got out in West Eaton Place and ran on foot into Eaton Terrace. Pursuing them was Police Constable March. They shot him in the stomach. Following him was Police Constable Sayer. They shot him in the leg. The hunt was on. Into Chester Terrace, down into South Eaton Place. At Gerald Road police station the police who were off duty rushed out. The murderers were now in Ebury Street being chased by police and public.

And then there was very nearly the first lynching to take place in London for a hundred years, because the crowd knew that these were the two men who had killed an English hero. A great cry of: 'Kill the bastards,' went up, and the police, after they had shown great courage and pertinacity, having arrested the two men, had to defend them from the anger of the crowd. It was touch and go. At one time it looked as if the two young men—they were both twenty-four—'John O'Brien' and 'James Connelly'[1] would indeed be trampled and torn to bits by the crowd,

1. The assumed names they were charged under.

but it was not to be. Perhaps the fury of the crowd abated. Perhaps they realised that it was not for them to murder the murderers. Perhaps the courage and determination of the police had its effect, but whatever the reason, the police were able to take the men who had been roughly handled back to their station and charge them with the murder of the Field Marshal.

The political result of the murder was catastrophic. Two years later, when the writer, as President of the Union, invited Mr. De Valera to speak in a debate at the Cambridge Union on the new Ireland the Vice-Chancellor, perhaps for the first time, intervened and forbade the invitation, which had to be cancelled. Perhaps he was wrong. Had Mr. De Valera come to England at that time and spoken in Cambridge it could well be that the young men, more forgiving or less involved than their elders, might have extended him a welcome and if they had done so the years of bitterness and frustration that were to follow in the relations between England and Ireland might well have been avoided, but the incident shows that the murder of the Field Marshal had made the English Establishment turn against the Irish with dislike and contempt.

The two prisoners, Reginald Dunne and Joseph O'Sullivan, had both served in the war. O'Sullivan was a cripple and had achieved the rank of lance corporal. Dunne had become a corporal. Both men had excellent characters. They were not in any sense members of the criminal class. They were cold-blooded political murderers. Their trial does not, I think, show English justice at its best, but it does perhaps show it at its most typical. Joseph O'Sullivan and Reginald Dunne were tried at the Central Criminal Court—the Old Bailey. They were defended by Artemus Jones, a Welsh Nationalist, who had much sympathy with the Irish cause. The judge was Mr. Justice Shearman, a careful and respected judge but never a strong or decisive one. The team for the prosecution included the Attorney General and Travers Humphreys. The legal cast indicated that this would be a great occasion.

The clerk of the court called first on Dunne and said:
'You are charged with the murder of Sir Henry Wilson. Are you guilty or not guilty?'

Dunne replied quietly: 'I admit shooting Sir Henry Wilson.'

The clerk then repeated his question:

'Are you guilty or not guilty of the murder of Sir Henry Wilson?'

To this Dunne replied:

'That is all I can say.'

The judge intervened and said: 'Unless he says "Guilty" I shall treat it as a plea of "Not guilty".'

This, of course, was perfectly correct.

The clerk then addressed O'Sullivan:

'Are you guilty or not guilty of the murder of Sir Henry Wilson?'

O'Sullivan replied: 'I admit shooting him, sir.'

Again the judge, correctly, took this to be a plea of not guilty.

The evidence, of course, was overwhelming and included the medical evidence of that strange and brilliant man Dr. Bernard Spilsbury, who was later to die by his own hand. After the prosecution had closed their case the judge explained to the jury that the accused did not have to go into the witness box unless they wished to, but if they did so they could be cross-examined on whatever they said. If they went into the witness box their statements would have to be on oath. If they chose to remain in the dock they could make a statement from there to the jury which would not be on oath and which would not be subject to cross-examination, though he, the judge, might comment on it on his summing-up.

Artemus Jones then said one of the prisoners, Dunne, wished to read a statement. He handed to the clerk of the court three sheets of paper given him by the prisoner, Dunne. The clerk of the court handed the statement to Mr. Justice Shearman. The judge read it carefully and then said: 'I cannot allow this to be read. It is a political manifesto. It is not a defence or a plea in mitigation. As I understand this document it is an attempt to justify the murder and as it is a political manifesto I cannot allow it.'

Artemus Jones asked for a brief adjournment so that he could consider the situation that had arisen and this was granted. A quarter of an hour later defence counsel returned to court, the judge taking his seat on the Bench again.

Artemus Jones rose and said: 'My Lord, in the face of your refusal to allow the document to be read, the prisoners do not wish to be legally represented and they have withdrawn their instructions to us. In these circumstances there is no course open to Counsel than to withdraw from the case.'

The judge was then at some pains to make it quite clear that he was not preventing the prisoners making a statement from the dock, but he was forbidding the reading of 'this political manifesto'.

Artemus Jones said: 'I appreciate your Lordship's point of view, but I am acting as spokesman for the prisoners and derive my authority only from them. If they withdraw that authority I have no alternative but to withdraw from the case. I ask your Lordship to allow the solicitor for Dunne to have the statement back.'

The judge, however, took the view that as Mr. Artemus Jones had retired from the case he could no longer be 'heard'.

The judge then addressed the prisoners and again said to them: 'You are now representing yourselves and may go into the witness box if you wish, but if you do you will be cross-examined by Counsel. On the other hand, if you do not wish to give evidence on oath you can make a statement relative to this matter from where you are.'

Both prisoners said that they did not wish to go into the witness box but that Dunne would make a statement from the dock. Dunne then addressed the jury in these words:

'I suppose I must cut out the patriotic adjectives that I feel inclined to use under the present circumstances, but

I must state that I feel still, under those very circumstances, proudly conscious that I am an Irishman. You
have heard all the accounts from the Divisional Inspector
who has been asked for accounts of my character, and
you will agree that this is the first time that I, and my
friend, for that matter, have appeared in any criminal
court. That I take a particular pride in, besides my national pride in being a member of the Irish race. I have
endeavoured to give an honest statement of the matter
from a national point of view, but it seems that privilege
is denied me. I, for my part, am sorry that you, as members of the jury, are denied the chance of hearing an honest
Irishman's statement. Several of you, I have no doubt,
endeavoured to do your best in the recent great European
war. I also took my share in that war, fighting for the
principles for which this country stood. Those principles,
I found, as an Irishman, were not applied to my own
country, and I have endeavoured to strike a blow for it.'

This statement was, of course, a perfectly proper one.
In effect, it merely said: 'We are men of good character.'
But the crime of murder, which is the most horrible of all
crimes and the greatest crime in the criminal calendar
except treason, is often committed by people of hitherto
good character. It is a crime which in England formerly
the criminal classes sought to avoid and therefore the plea of good character in a murder charge is not
of great force as it would be, for instance, in a charge of
larceny or fraud. What is interesting is to compare the
statement that Reginald Dunne made with the statement
that he wished to read and which the judge disallowed on
the pretext that it was a political manifesto.

Personally, reading the statement now, I do not think it
was entirely a political manifesto. For instance, there
were charges against the prisoners of attempting to murder the police as well as of murdering Sir Henry Wilson
and in the statement they point out that they were not
firing to kill but to escape arrest. And then again there is a
direct reference to their character and their war service.

Further on they explain how the Irish saw Sir Henry Wilson as the brains behind the Orange Terror. The statement continues with allegations of British atrocities in Ireland, although these statements might be said to constitute a political manifesto, surely they could also be interpreted as a plea in mitigation of sentence, the suggestion being that the prisoners had done what they did after being unbearably provoked. And even the plea that they had been willing to die in the war for liberty and then found no liberty in Ireland was a matter that the jury might have wished to hear. On reflection it would seem that Mr. Justice Shearman would have been wiser to allow this statement to have been read for, as the old saying goes, justice must not only be done but must be seen to be done.

The statement, in fact, was of great interest, much of it extremely specious and even persuasive, but nevertheless evoking the deeply held emotions of the time.

This was the statement that the jury did not hear.

'My Lord and Members of the Jury, my friend and I stand here before you today charged with the offence of murder and I have no doubt that from the evidence placed before you by the prosecution you will find us both guilty. With regard to the charges of attempted murder, we merely fired, as everyone must know, to try and escape arrest.

'The offence of murder is a very serious matter, and any act which results in the loss of human life requires very grave and substantial reasons. We have never until now been charged with any crime. As you have heard from the police officer who gave evidence as to our characters and our previous records, we have both been men in the British Army. We both joined voluntarily for the purpose of taking human life, in order that the principles for which this country stood should be upheld and preserved. Those principles, we were told, were Self-Determination and Freedom for Small Nations. We both, as I have said, fought for those principles, and we were commended for doing so, and I imagine that several of you gentlemen of the Jury did likewise. We came back from France to find that Self-Determination had been given to some nations we had never heard of, but that it had been denied in Ireland. We found, on the contrary, that our country was being divided into two countries; that a government had been set up for the Belfast district, and that under that government outrages were being perpetrated that are a disgrace to civilisation—many of the outrages being committed by men in uniform and in the pay of the Belfast government. We took our part in supporting the aspirations of our fellow countrymen, in the same way as we took part in supporting the nations of the world who fought for the rights of small nationalities.

'Who was Sir Henry Wilson, what was his policy, and what did he stand for? You have all read in the newspapers lately and been told that he was a great British Field Marshal, but his activities in other fields are unknown to the bulk of the British public. The nation to which we have the honour to belong, the Irish nation, knew him, not so much as the great British Field Marshal, but as the man behind what is known in Ireland as the Orange Terror. He was at the time of his death the Military Adviser to what is colloquially called the Ulster government, and as Military Adviser he raised and organised a body of men known as the Ulster Special Constables, who are the principal agents in his campaign of terrorism.

'My Lord and Members of the Jury, I do not propose to go into details of the horrible outrages committed on men and women and children of my race in Belfast and other places in the jurisdiction of the Ulster government. Among Irishmen it is well known that about five hundred men, women and children have been killed within the last few months, nearly two thousand wounded, and not one offender brought to justice. More than nine thousand persons have been expelled from their employment and twenty-three thousand men, women and children driven from their homes. All the big cities of this country, and even those of Northern France, are now receiving these refugees. Sir Henry Wilson was the representative figure and the organiser of the system that made these things possible.

'At his suggestion and advice the Ulster Parliament passed an Act authorising the flogging of political opponents, and this power is now exercised and enforced by the courts in Ulster.

'There is and can be no political liberty in a country where one political party outrages, oppresses and intimidates not only its political opponents, but persons whose religious opinions differ from the party in power. The same principle for which we shed our blood on the battlefield of Europe led us to commit the act we are charged with.

'My Lords and Members of the Jury, you can condemn us to death today, but you cannot deprive us of the belief that what we have done was necessary to preserve the lives, the homes and the happiness of our countrymen in Ireland. You may by your verdict find us guilty, but we will go to the scaffold justified by the verdict of our consciences.'

There could be but one conclusion to the case. Both prisoners were sentenced to death, to be hanged by the neck until they were dead, in the good old-fashioned way.

Artemus Jones appealed on behalf of the prisoners and the Bench in the Court of Appeal included the loquacious and allegedly witty Mr. Justice Darling and Mr. Justice Branson, one of the best judges of the century. They upheld Mr. Justice Shearman, taking the view that not only had he acted within his discretion in refusing to allow the statement to be read but that he actually had a duty to act in this way.

Both the prisoners were executed at Wandsworth Prison, facing death without flinching. They will live in the records of England for their iniquity, and in the legend of Ireland for their courage.

9

The Assassination of General Lim

SIAM, which we now call Thailand, is unique among the nations of South-East Asia. It has always been a monarchy from time immemorial and with the exception of a brief period of Burmese conquest it has always been free.

Today the city of Bangkok is modern, progressive, booming, alive with air-conditioned hotels and the continual roar of traffic that indicate the current prosperity of the country which, as of old, exports rice, teak, and tin to the markets of the world. The King still reigns in Bangkok, but today he is a modern-minded young monarch with a very beautiful queen and a charming family. The Thai people and government support the policies of the United States in South-East Asia and, while remaining sturdily independent, they have the advantage of being protected by the golden umbrella of American power.

The assassination of General Lim belongs to another era in Thailand when the country was still called Siam, when the King ruled in Bangkok as absolute monarch and when the feudal princes of the North, the Chow Luangs of Chiengmai, Lampoon, Nan, Lampang and Phrae, had considerable influence in their own territories over the Lao people who were their subjects and who were the northern branch of the Siamese race, speaking a language that was similar but in many respects different. Consequently a young judge from Bangkok, sitting in the court in Chiengmai, although he might understand the evidence of a local official, might not be able to understand evidence given by a woman from the country. The supreme King in Bangkok, in these days, seldom if ever visited the North, where the Lao princes were regarded as 'Tigers in the Jungle'.

Today the young King and his family often visit the North, which is regarded as a delightful holiday resort, and Bangkok and Chiengmai are linked by an excellent highway as well as by the railway, but in the days of which I am now going to speak there was no road nor was there any railway and, of course, no air link. The journey from Chiengmai to Bangkok took approximately six weeks, first by raft to Paknampoh, then by river steamer to Bangkok. Six weeks is a long time and many things can happen during such an interval, for instance a man could be assassinated and his body could be cremated and he could be forgotten, passing into that long yesterday which the Buddhists regard as a story which has been told and is sometimes better unremembered.

I was posted to the International Court in Chiengmai in 1931 while the absolute monarchy was still reigning in Bangkok, the all-important fact of Siamese life. The situation was entrancingly simple. The business of the nation was conducted by the King with his Ministers on one afternoon each week. There were no arguments. The King's written or spoken word was law. The Ministers were responsible for their ministries, but they did not have to think about policy for that had already been decided for them. There was one terrifying crime in Siam and that was the crime of treason. It very rarely occurred but when it did, in whatever guise, it was suppressed with vigour. Those who had attempted to plot against the throne were executed and in the old days their families, too, were blotted out. It was true that the King then on the throne had been educated abroad, in fact at Eton, but he was still, on state occasions, carried on his palanquin by his nobles; he still retained white elephants as the eternal symbol of Eastern majesty and his word was still law.

Democracy may be the best form of government but it is certainly the most difficult. Absolutism makes things run smoothly. There were no 'politics' in Siam. There was only one English-language paper, which was extremely loyal and discreet. It was edited by an old Scotsman of great character. Over the warm sunny valleys of Siam the sun shone in its Eastern grandeur and, although no one was very rich, except, of course, the King and his relatives, no one was too poor. The sun provided eternal warmth, the rivers provided pure water, rice grew in the rich mud of the Menam river almost for the asking, a house could be built by a man and his wife with bamboo and an attap roof and from the rivers came a free and plentiful supply of fish.

The mornings and the evenings were delightful in Siam, the mornings as fresh and brilliant as a newly minted coin, and the evenings as smooth and lustrous as a velvet dress. True, the days were apt to be hot except in the short winter of December and January, but they were bearable, for the climate of Siam was temperate for a tropical country. There was never the blazing torrid heat of the Indian and African continental climate, and during the autumn months rain would fall, sometimes torrentially but more frequently for an hour or two, rather in the manner of an English June. The monsoon was unknown in Siam.

When I was posted to Chiengmai I noticed the difference immediately, for the impression I had was that I had left behind me for good the busy, bustling life that centred round Bangkok and had passed through the looking glass into a serene and seductive country where the air sparkled like champagne and the people smiled with the very joy of living. There were mountains here and great green forests and the rivers raced through gorges, but the people had an air of great content and always an air of leisure so that one knew that time was no longer important.

I had not been in the North very long when I discovered

that the serenity, although it was so attractive, clothed an underlying aspect of violence. These were a gay and happy people, yes, but beneath the surface the dagger and the gun could still speak violently and suddenly. For here in the North grew opium and opium has always meant not only dreams of bliss but dreams of death.

The house that had been secured for me in Chiengmai was near the American Mission compound and was built of stone surrounded by a broad verandah. There were, of course, no glass window-panes, for these would have made the house unbearably hot. There were merely wooden shutters which were closed and locked at night when a watchman sat outside in a wicker chair, nursing a long bamboo pole with which he was supposed to chase away any thieves who might materialise during the night. The kitchen was about fifty yards from the house along a covered cement alleyway. The floors of the house were made of teak taken from the extensive teak forests, some of which were worked by the Siamese themselves but most of which were leased to Danish, British and French firms. It was an attractive little house in about two acres of garden and had two entrances, the rear entrance opening on to a lane that joined the main road past a saw mill, and the front entrance that joined the same road after running for some way along the white wall of a Buddhist temple.

We had, apart from the cook who was Chinese, an ayah and two women who ran the house. There was also a driver of my car and one gardener who sat in the shade of a banana tree sleeping gently until I returned from court when he would spring into the most unlikely activity. Flowers grew in the garden very abundantly. Orchids which are tough and prolific when grown in a warm climate did extremely well and flowers like zinnias, petunias and phlox did very well in the winter months from about November to March. April was the hottest month of the year and during that month the courts closed so that we were free to go and spend the time at our bungalow on

Doi Sutep, the five-thousand-foot mountain that rose splendidly from the plain about three miles from the town of Chiengmai itself.

My work was not too difficult. It consisted in trying with two Siamese judges any cases that came before the court that involved British subjects. This did not only include people from Britain, it also included all the Indians living in the North and quite a large number of Burmese. Legally these were the only people over whom I had any jurisdiction but the Siamese judges used to be worried and, I think, a little embarrassed if foreigners of other nationalities came before them and for this reason I was asked to sit in any cases that involved Europeans and Americans. It was thought that if they were given the same facilities as the British they could not possibly complain and a great deal of trouble might be avoided. In the Siam I am speaking of the avoidance of trouble was a fine art.

Siamese society was strictly stratified in two main streams, one headed by the King, contained the various ranks of the princes, and the other, equally headed by the King, contained all the officials from the highest grade to the lowest. The highest official in Chiengmai was the Tessa or Viceroy. In fact the house where we lived, although it belonged to a Chinese (who also owned the neighbouring saw mill), had been let as a private residence to the former Viceroy, Prince Bowaradet, who later was to lead an abortive royal coup against the military government that was to seize power in June 1932. The Prince very nearly succeeded in his design. Had he done so the pattern of Siamese history during the last thirty years might have been quite different, but in the event the effect was to turn the monarchy from an absolute rule into a constitutional rule. This again was amended to give all the prestige to the monarchy and to give power to a military government that ruled with considerable moderation and wisdom. After seven hundred years of absolute monarchy Siam was not ripe for Western-style democracy.

European life settled into a very easy groove that centred on the Gymkhana Club in the evenings. The Gymkhana Club was a very simple affair, the clubhouse being a pleasant little attap-roofed building and the land enclosing four tennis courts, two squash courts and a nine-hole golf course. One of the more energetic members of the club committee wrote a letter to the *Field* asking whether the layout of the golf course could be improved and this led to one of those epic British debates during which a sketch of the golf course was reproduced in that newspaper and everyone from bishops to golf architects had their say. After this the course remained exactly as it was before.

I suppose that in the resident comr·unity we were perhaps a hundred and fifty people, but .any of the husbands would be out working in the teak forests and they only returned from time to time on a few days' leave. The American missionaries were too busy teaching and doctoring for the vast area of the North to play much part in social life and the active community which went each evening to the Gymkhana Club for exercise was mainly British. There were two Consulates in Chiengmai, the British and the French, but as the French Consul smoked opium he was not always with us and the British Consul and a retired consular official, who had been given the rank of Consul General on retirement, were the leaders of the British community. The Consul, who was a stout, florid middle-aged man was a very decent fellow but took his position very seriously, regarding himself as the direct representative of King George in the north of Siam.

There was one other social network in Chiengmai and that was the family of the ruling Prince called Chow Luang. This old gentleman was greatly venerated by the local people, but in fact anyone in authority received a great deal of courteous attention which we would now regard as being exaggerated or odd. For instance, when I drove out of my gate in the morning the children playing in the road would run and kneel in the ditches that lined it, raising their hands palm to palm up to their foreheads in salutation.

The family of the Prince were delightful people, if a little arbitrary by modern standards. For instance, the old man himself when he had to attend a function quite near to his palace to which there was no convenient road had his blue Daimler driven across country through the fences of the farmers so that he should arrive not more than a quarter of an hour late. This was regarded as perfectly normal and the farmers concerned re-erected their fences quite amicably and cheerfully.

During the first six months I was in Chiengmai hardly a rustle appeared on the smooth smiling surface of the countryside. Chiengmai itself was a busy little town and quite a number of handcrafts persisted there, for instance the making of black and gold lacquer trays and bowls, and, of course, at Lampoon, nearby, there was the weaving of Thai silk, not yet a large industry. The price of the best Thai silk was about five shillings a yard. It has gone up since.

The community at the Gymkhana Club got to know each other very well. It included two terrific elderly gentlemen, both Scottish, one of whom had been manager of the Bombay-Burma Trading Corporation and the other manager of the Borneo Company. They both had Siamese wives and very large families and because of, or in spite of, this they had remained incurably British, for instance, their breakfasts consisted of Scotch oatmeal, rashers of ham and eggs, coffee, toast and marmalade. This was not the breakfast of the local population, who ate a soft rice dish in the morning in which vegetables and possibly fish or meat had been mixed.

Both these men were extremely well informed and it was from one of them, Alexander Bruce, that I first heard that a General Lim was going to visit us. Lim? Lim? Chinese, surely? 'Yes, I think he was a war lord or something of that kind. Made his pile in China. Got it out and is going to settle down here. Intends to build a house near Doi Sutep.'

Ten days later General Lim arrived with two young wives, one elderly wife, the senior lady, a son who followed him everywhere, always walking a few feet behind his father, and several retainers who would lurk about at a discreet distance but whose job obviously was to protect their lord and master, though why General Lim should think that he needed protection in this peaceful backwater no one could fathom. Perhaps it was that in his own dangerous country he had become used to having a bodyguard and felt unhappy without it. This is quite possible. I remember myself in Siam many years later in 1946 becoming accustomed to sleeping with a revolver under my pillow. This was a relic of the war years and was quite unnecessary, but two or three years later, when I abandoned the habit, I missed it and used to grope for the gun that was not there. We are all creatures of habit.

The most addictive of all habits, the opium habit, was not common in Chiengmai and was almost confined to the hill farmers who grew the crop. I think General Lim smoked opium but in moderation, as the Chinese are able to do. His underlip was somewhat pendulous. His skin a little tightly drawn over his face and it had the bloom of a fresh peach. His eyes were sometimes lacklustre but at other times bright and animated and all these aspects are characteristic of the moderate opium-smoker. This did not prevent him being a man of imposing appearance and natural authority. He was immediately elected a member of the Gymkhana Club and used to come most evenings and have a drink, accompanied by his two young wives who appeared to dote on him. He got on very well with the British members because he could talk about the things they understood, such as horses and the teak forests. He resolutely refused to play any games, saying, darkly, 'I have all the exercise I need.' General Lim started to build his house, having bought about five acres of land on the road between the town and the mountain.

In Chiengmai we usually dined about half past eight or nine and I recall with pleasure that we still had in the dining-room a punkah which stirred the air in a leisurely kind of way and was pulled from outside by a servant who had nothing better to do. We seldom had visitors in the evening unless we were going out to dinner or had guests coming to dine at our house. It was therefore surprising when we were taking coffee on the verandah one evening that a car should come down the drive and out of it should step General Lim, followed by his son who never spoke. I thought at first he might be a mute, but he was not. Presumably he believed that silence was golden. General Lim came in and shook hands and very gently, almost imperceptibly, he raised one eyebrow. I took this to mean that what he had to say to me was for my ears alone, and my wife, discerning this, smiled and withdrew.

'I find it a little difficult to tell you what I have to say but the fact is that my life was in great danger and, well, I should like to live.'

I did not think this called for any comment. We all preferred to live, if possible. Clearly General Lim had not yet decanted the cream in the coconut. I think perhaps he was a little disappointed that I did not show more curiosity but he continued with composure:

'During the time I had my province in China one of my duties was to export the opium we grew in the hills and it was from this trade that I was able to save the modest pittance—' General Lim smiled deprecatingly '—that has enabled me to come to this delightful country and settle down here. Unfortunately my enemies—one always makes enemies in the opium business—appear to have followed me here and I think they have employed local people to murder me.' The General paused.

I thought it would be polite at this point if I assisted the General with a question, so I said: 'How do you know this, General?'

'Because of this.' He drew a paper from his pocket and

handed it to me. It was in English and the message was a simple one and absolutely clear. It said: 'You are to die on the third day of the Chinese New Year.'

I looked at the General. 'But that is in ten days' time,' I said.

The General nodded gravely, and his son, who had not spoken a word, took a pinch of snuff from a gold snuff-box which he carried in the right-hand pocket of his silk tunic coat.

'You want the Siamese to protect you?'

'I do not know whether they can do this, but I thought that you might give me some advice.'

'I think the police should be informed immediately and if you like I will suggest that they give you a guard night and day, in addition to your own retainers.'

General Lim and his son looked at one another and the son bowed gravely to his father, who apparently valued his opinion.

'We are grateful to you,' said General Lim. He got up and again looked at his son, who produced from the other pocket of his coat a sapphire ring which he handed to me.

'A small present for your wife.' The General bowed and shook hands. The son bowed and they left, entering their car and disappearing into the night. I decided to drop in at the police station on my way to court in the morning. It might all be a hoax, some kind of very bad joke, but I felt that the General took it seriously. Obviously, dealing in opium in his own country he had fallen foul of his competitors. I should think that he had been a fairly ruthless man. In fact I do not think at this time one would have survived as a Chinese war lord without being ruthless.

I informed Major Pravit, the head of police, of the General's request and he said he would do something about it. I thought no more about the matter until the last day of the Chinese New Year, which also happened to be the birthday of the King's uncle. The British Consul gave a reception on the delightful lawn of the Consulate by the river. General Lim was one of the guests. His son followed him everywhere, but he had left both his personal guard and his police guard outside, assuming that he would be perfectly safe within the gates of His Britannic Majesty.

It was a false assumption. After a certain amount of champagne had been drunk, but just before the toast of the King's uncle was proposed, three men came in by the gate, the first was a police captain, the second a sergeant and the third a constable. They walked up to General Lim and I had no doubt that they were the guard who had been assigned to him, but things in Siam are not always what they seem, for the captain drew a gun from his holster and shot General Lim three times through the heart. He died there and then. The sergeant then executed his son. The constable covered the retreat of the other two men with a gun, obviously loaded. Wisely, if not very bravely, no one stirred. The three men vanished.

The bodies of General Lim and his son were carried into the building and the party drank champagne a little faster until the royal toast had been proposed. On my way back I dropped in again at the police station, but, of course, they had never heard of the three men who had murdered the General and his son. They had been impostors wearing Siamese police uniform.

The riddle of General Lim's murder was never cleared up. The three men had vanished into thin air, which only shows how dangerous it is to enter the opium trade. Incidentally, it is as dangerous today as it was then. I was genuinely sorry, for I liked General Lim. He was really anxious to retire and spend his remaining days with his two beautiful young wives in the peaceful little town of Chiengmai. It was extremely bad luck that his enemies in China should have for him such an implacable and determined hatred.

10

Winter in Washington

JUST before Christmas in a fashionable street in Washington two men were walking towards each other. Their eyes met and the eyes of one man filled with hatred and those of the other with fear. The man who was afraid was an imposing figure, tall, strong, ugly but commanding. The man who was angry had a clever, sensitive, handsome face. He took a revolver from his coat pocket and emptied the magazine into the stomach and heart of the big man, who died, there and then, on the pavement, his breath still showing in the frosty morning air.

The man who was assassinated was Phillip Barton Key, Attorney General and leader of the Washington Bar. The man who killed him, Daniel Sickles, had been First Secretary of the American Embassy in London but had returned to his own country to pursue a legal and political career which he was doing with great success, having become in the space of a year or so one of the best-known advocates in Washington and having been returned as a member of Congress at the turn of the century.

I spoke of Phillip Barton Key as Attorney General but his actual Office was District Attorney for Columbia. This office entailed duties roughly corresponding to those of the Attorney General in Britain, but the office in the United States was subject to political pressures which the equivalent office in England is not.

Key was an extraordinary-looking man over six foot four in height with a build of a wrestler. His mouth had a twist and this added to the menace of his eyes which were very deep-set and gave him a strange appearance. He was almost startlingly ugly, but it was not a revolting ugliness. It might be an attractive ugliness. It seemed to reflect immense physical power and his face also indicated a passionate determination.

So Daniel Sickles had murdered Phillip Barton Key in a public place in Washington. He did not deny it. He was put on trial and the trial became a great *cause célèbre* of American history, but it was what had gone before that titillated, excited and enthralled Washington society, because Phillip Barton Key had for over a year been the lover of Mrs. Sickles, and it was only after he had discovered this fact that Sickles had decided that Key must die.

Mrs. Sickles was Italian and she was quite lovely. She had a delicate and delicious figure, dark brown eyes that sparkled with the joy of living and her mouth was full and very red. She was, perhaps, the ambitious American man's idea of the wife who would preside with infinite distinction at their dinner parties, winning him friends from other influential men and establishing him as a man of the future. Daniel Sickles was very proud of his wife's tact and diplomacy. She could put any one at their ease, especially men, but she was almost equally good with women, who are easily diverted. She was gay, amusing and unmalicious. She seemed to assume that other women were as lovely and as well endowed as she was herself and this was not too indirect a form of flattery.

As for men, they could not resist her. She had an Italian accent which they listened to entranced. She was the exact opposite of the blonde, athletic American type of young wife. She brought to the men who visited their house the warmth and colour and animation of her homeland. When they saw her they felt that this was going to be a tremendous evening and that they were very lucky to be asked to the Sickles' house. Moreover, clearly Mrs. Sickles was devoted to her clever and ambitious husband. This made it much more pleasant for visiting dignitaries. They kept telling themselves what a lucky man Daniel Sickles was. The verdict of Washington society on the Sickles family was that they were the most captivating married couple of the moment and, obviously, ideally happy.

Nor was this public verdict so far out until one day Daniel Sickles appeared for the defence in a case in which Phillip Barton Key was prosecuting. Sickles secured the acquittal of his client and, perhaps to soften the blow for the District Attorney, and as it was already late, he said: 'Why don't you come to my house for some supper? I know my wife will have something ready.'

As it happened Key had nothing to do that night. So he accepted.

As soon as the delicate and laughing Mrs. Sickles saw Phillip Barton Key she knew that this dominating-looking man with the immense physique held an irresistible attraction for her, but she was a clever woman and she used the usual method by which women are able to conceal their real feelings even from those closest to them. If she exerted herself that evening even more than usual, if her smile was even more seductive and her gaiety less restrained, well, no doubt that was because Key was a very important man indeed, certainly in the legal world, and he was entitled to the full treatment. Key enjoyed the evening enormously and Daniel Sickles thanked his wife for making another conquest, another man who would help Sickles along the tough and sometimes crooked road that led to a governorship or perhaps even higher than that.

Within three months Key had become Mrs. Sickles' lover and their routine was to drive out into the country away from Washington and to forget. Key told Mrs. Sickles that he was prepared to give up everything in order to marry her and she assured him that she too would sacrifice everything for him. Both sides had a lot to give up.

Key had his great position at the Bar, not easily won, the prize seized at last after long years of rough court-room victories and some unforgettable defeats. Mrs. Sickles had just as much to forsake, for it was generally thought that Daniel Sickles was in a class by himself, an abler man than Key, possibly less ruthless, but not less ambitious. His success after returning from London had been phenomenal. He obviously had supreme self-confidence. No man not entirely sure of himself would have given up the Diplomatic Service when within a few years he knew that he would be offered a post as Ambassador in some fairly important country. Daniel Sickles gave it up without a thought, confident that he could capture Washington with the help of his beautiful wife. He was right. Washington society, both official and unofficial, fell for the Sickles. They were 'in'. The President himself was watching the career of this immensely promising young man with kindly interest.

Both the lovers must have realised that they were throwing aside a future of wealth and influence, but they did not hesitate. This was one of the rare cases in which some peculiar alchemy of the body and the spirit drove out all thoughts of discretion.

Remarkably enough, for many months Sickles knew nothing of what was going on. He was such a busy man, so intent on success, and success was coming to him so serenely and so surely that Theresa Sickles was able to keep the truth from her husband without too much difficulty. Then, of course, one day the inevitable anonymous letter was left mysteriously on the mantelpiece of Daniel Sickles' study. He opened it and read: 'Your wife has been the lover of Key for months. They meet at a house in Fifteenth Street which belongs to Key. It has a Negro caretaker and your wife knows when Key is in because a piece of black cord hangs from the second-story front window.'

The writer added a great deal of circumstantial detail and the lawyer read it very carefully. He was immensely experienced in penetrating evidence of this kind and tearing out the fact from the fiction. He hated to believe what he read but as a lawyer he could not reject the accumulated circumstantial detail of the letter. In his office next day he instructed his clerk to find out who rented the house at the far right-hand corner of Fifteenth Street.

Next day the clerk said: 'The tenant of the house you spoke about, sir, it is Mr. Key.'

He went straight home and faced his wife. Theresa denied everything. She had never heard of the house on Fifteenth Street. She had never been for drives in the country with Key. She had never, of course, allowed him to make love to her. It was all a plot by people who were jealous of her husband and perhaps, who knows, also engineered by some woman who was jealous of her. For a moment Sickles was taken aback. With the letter in his hand, and the knowledge that he had, he had expected her to confess, but she denied it entirely.

The temptation to accept what she said must have been considerable, for he loved her and if he could believe her he was safe. But could he believe her? He read the letter again there and then and decided she was lying.

Then followed what must have been one of the most extraordinary private trials between a husband and wife. Daniel Sickles was a master of cross-examination. His method was the classic one of putting to the witness everything that was virtually admitted and piling up the evidence step by step until in the end the witness was faced with the final logical but terrifying questions to which in reality there was no reply. Daniel Sickles subjected his wife to this technique and for over an hour she refused to be broken, but in the end she began to contradict herself. She began to make wild and unnecessary allegations. She began to twist and turn. At last she fell on the floor, sobbing bitterly, and saying: 'It is all true. It is just as you say.'

Theresa, during her ordeal, made out a case for herself.

She failed, of course, to establish her innocence, but she did persuade her husband that she had been hypnotised and carried off her feet by Key, that she had not wanted to submit to him at first but had been swept along by his ruthless determination to capture her. Daniel Sickles was inclined to believe this, but he demanded back his wedding ring and insisted on Theresa's mother taking her away. Theresa left for her own family and it was probably this fact that led to the assassination of Key, for the house that had been filled with laughter and a certain warm loveliness was now empty and desolate, a wrecked home. In it Daniel Sickles was alone with his thoughts and they were thoughts of the utmost bitterness. What could he do? His private life had been wrecked irretrievably. True, his public life remained, but without Theresa he did not have the same appetite for it.

He brooded at home for many days, refusing to see anyone, and then one morning a great and irresistible anger welled up inside him, He had two guns in the house. Carefully and methodically he filled the magazine of one gun and slipped it into his pocket. He had decided that Key must die.

It was a cold-blooded assassination, in fact an execution, almost an act of judicial retribution. Key apparently knew that he was going to die when he saw the look on Daniel Sickles' face. At that moment he had less than thirty seconds to live.

The trial created immense interest. Sickles was defended by Henry Stanton, one of the great advocates of his day. Stanton was up against formidable difficulties. Had Sickles killed Key when he first discovered his wife's adultery then the law would have been more favourable, because it can be held that a man, suddenly overcome by an overpowering passion and rightful indignation, may be excused acts which would otherwise be inexcusable. But Daniel Sickles had not struck in the hot anger of discovery. He had waited. He had waited many days, turning over the matter in his mind. He had sent his wife away and still he had not struck, and then one day he had decided with the utmost deliberation to kill Key.

Now how could this possibly be justified? How could it not be murder? For here was 'malice aforethought' long weighed and deliberately planned. Here was motive, strong, admitted. Here was a virtual confession—none of the facts in dispute. From the point of view of cold logical law here was murder indeed.

The best that Daniel Sickles could hope for, according to the dictates of law, was a verdict of guilty, at least of murder in a minor degree with a recommendation from the jury pleading the gross provocation as an extenuating circumstance.

It is often said that in France the crime of passion is treated with peculiar leniency. I doubt if this is so. French juries may be in favour of love, but they are usually most averse to murder and French judges are a cold and logical race, not easily stirred by warm rhetoric or passionate pleas for mercy. And in France, too, there is no tradition of the gun, for the French, whether we like them or not, have been a civilised race for a very long time and, apart from the outbreak of sadistic fury that accompanied the French Revolution, the rule of law has been maintained in France and the gangster, the gunman, and indeed every killer, sternly discouraged.

In America, certainly in the United States, the tradition is somewhat different. Although by and large the American law of murder is founded on the old English laws of homicide, the American public have always had, in a diminishing degree, a law of their own. They have always been reluctant to hand over to the judicature and to the law officers complete control in affairs of killing. Until very recently the rare lynchings that occurred were the manifest sign of this reluctance. Lynchings now have stopped, or almost stopped, but American juries are still apt, on occasion, to take the law into their own hands and to ignore judical direction. They are encouraged to do this by very strong and direct public pressure.

For instance, when Daniel Sickles was put on trial a specially secured dock, which was in fact an iron cage, was built to hold him, not that the authorities feared any violence from him but because they suspected or knew that, if he was convicted, his friends and supporters would attempt to rescue him, to snatch him out of the terrible position he was in and to give him his liberty. But public opinion was not entirely with Daniel Sickles. The dead man, too, had his influential friends who said that murder must meet its just reward.

So that when Henry Stanton finished his great speech for the defence—he spoke for over eight hours—and the jury retired the issue was still very much in doubt. There were those who believed that an acquittal was quite impossible because the judge had directed the jury that they should convict and leave the exercise of leniency to the authorities whose job it was to investigate that aspect of the case. The supporters of Daniel Sickles were equally convinced that, come what may, their man would be acquitted. He had suffered a deadly indignity. He had executed a man who deserved to die. If ever a murder could be justified then murder was justified in this case.

The jury were out for an hour and twenty-five minutes and they must have been long minutes for Daniel Sickles. When they returned neither the foreman nor the other eleven jurors revealed anything at all by their expression. The foreman stood up and was asked what their verdict was? In a voice that contained no emotion whatever he answered, briskly: 'Not guilty.'

Sickles was mobbed by an immense crowd of supporters and admirers outside the court. They took the horses from his carriage and pulled it in triumph through wildly cheering crowds along the main street from the court. Sickles was free and Sickles was a hero. He forgave his wife, but she died within a year. During the Civil War Sickles became a major-general in the Northern army and lost a leg at Gettysburg. President Grant made him Ambassador in Spain and he conducted a brilliant and successful mission in Madrid. He found a new wife with whom he lived happily for many years and on his return to America filled a number of distinguished posts, including that of Civil Service Commissioner and Sheriff of New York City, a post that must have given him ironic satisfaction.

He was a brilliant conversationalist and to the end dominated any society in which he moved with his vivid tales of the American War and of battles in the courts. He died in New York at the age of ninety-three, having outlived by many years all his contemporaries in the great drama in which he had played a leading part.

That is the story of the assassination of Phillip Barton Key. But one question occurs to me which I have not seen answered before, and that question is: during the long period, alone in his house, while this brilliant man, with his razor-sharp legal mind, contemplated his past and his future, did he decide to take a calculated risk? Did he know that for certain when he had killed Key he would face a murder charge? Did he accept this and foresee that a great murder trial would follow and that, because of the nature of the case, and because of the custom of the country, he would be, in all probability, triumphantly acquitted? And, if he realised all this, did he decide to achieve the double target? Did he decide to murder the man he hated, knowing that he would be able to re-establish his own fortunes afterwards?

If Daniel Sickles was as deliberate and far-seeing a killer as this, then he stands out as the supreme example of the lawyer-murderer who killed, not so much in irresistible anger, as in cold implacable revenge.

II

The Waltham Blacks

HAVE you ever heard of the Waltham Blacks? I certainly had not. The title sounds something like a football team, but, although the Waltham Blacks were in a sense a sporting crowd, they assuredly did not play any ball game. They were responsible for a notorious assassination at Farnham Holt in the autumn of 1723 and that is what makes them our business. However, before we deal with the matter of their murder, it is, I think, interesting to know something of this weird brotherhood with their inordinate love of venison.

In the spring of 1722 a scribe, whose name we do not know, but who perhaps is sufficiently identified as a Country Gentleman, wrote to a friend in London this strange letter. Reading it one has to remind oneself that this all happened in England. The episode is so bizarre as to be almost incredible, but it is historically accurate.

Our friend the Country Gentleman had quite a gift for graphic description. This is what he wrote:

'Amongst the odd accidents which you know have happened to me in the course of a very unsettled life, I don't know any which has been more extraordinary, or surprising, than one I met with in going down to my own house, when I left you last in town. You cannot have heard of the Waltham Blacks, as they are called; a set of whimsical merry fellows, that are so mad to run the greatest hazards for the sake of a haunch of venison, and passing a jolly evening together. For my part, though the stories told of these people have reached my ears, yet I confess I took most of them for fables; and thought that, if there was truth in any of them, it was much exaggerated: but experience (the mistress of fools) has taught me the contrary, by the adventure I am going to relate; which, though it ended well enough at last, I confess at first put me a good deal out of humour.

'To begin, then: My horse got, some way, a stone in his foot, and therewith went so lame just as I entered the forest, that I really thought his shoulder slipped; finding it, however, impossible to get him along, I was even glad to take up with a little blind ale-house, which I perceived had a yard and a stable behind it. The man of the house received me very civilly, but when he perceived my horse was so lame, as scarcely to be able to stir a step, I observed he grew uneasy. I asked him whether I could lodge there that night; for I resolved not to spoil a horse which cost me twenty guineas, by riding him in such a condition. The man made no answer; we went into the house together; when I proposed the same question to the wife. She dealt more roughly and freely with me; saying, that truly I neither could nor should stay there, and was for hurrying her husband to get my horse out; however, on putting a crown into her hand, and promising her another for my lodging, she began to consider a little; and, at last, told me that there was indeed a little bed above stairs, on which she would order a clean pair of sheets to be put; for she was persuaded that I was more of a gentleman than to take any notice of what was passing there. This made me more uneasy than I was before. I concluded now that I had got into a den of highwaymen, and expected nothing less than to be robbed, and have my thoat cut into the bargain; however, finding there was no remedy, I even sat myself down, and endeavoured to be as easy as I could. By this time it had become very dark; and I heard three or four horsemen alight and lead their horses into the yard.

'As the men returned and were coming into the room where I sat, I overheard my landlord exclaiming, "Indeed, brother, you need not be uneasy; I am positive the gentleman's a man of honour!" To which I heard another voice reply, "What good could our deaths do a stranger? Faith I don't apprehend half the danger that you do. I dare say the gentleman would be glad of our company, and we should be pleased with his. Come, hang fear! I'll lead the way."

'So said, so done: in they came, five of them, all disguised so effectually, that I declare, unless it were in the same disguise, I should not be able to distinguish any of them. Down they sat, and he, who I supposed was constituted their captain "*pro hac vice*", accosted me with great civility, asking if I would honour them with my company to supper? I acknowledged. I did not yet guess the profession of my new acquaintances; but supposing my landlord would be cautious of suffering either a robbery or a murder in his own house, I knew not how, but, by degrees, my mind grew perfectly easy.

'About ten o'clock I heard a very great noise of horse, and soon after men's feet trampling in a room over my head: then my landlord came down, and informed us, supper was just ready to go upon the table.

'Upon this, we were all desired to walk up; and he, whom I before called the Captain, presented me, with a humorous kind of ceremony, to a man more disguised than the rest, who sat at the upper end of the table; telling me, at the same time, he hoped I would not refuse to pay my respects to PRINCE OROONOKO, King of the Blacks! It then immediately struck into my head who these worthy persons were, into whose company I had thus accidentally fallen. I called myself a thousand blockheads in my mind for not finding it out before; but the hurry of things, or to speak truth, the fear I was in, prevented my judging even from the most evident signs.

'As soon as this awkward ceremony had been ended, supper was brought in, which consisted of eighteen dishes of venison in every shape; roasted, boiled with broth, hashed collups, pasties, umble pies, and a large haunch in the middle, larded. The table we sat at was very large, and the company in all twenty-one persons; at each of our elbows, there was set a bottle of claret; and the man and woman of the house sat down at the lower end. Two or three of the fellows had got natural voices, and so the evening was spent as merrily as the rakes passed theirs at the King's Arms, or the City apprentices with their masters' maids at Sadler's Wells.

'About two, the company seemed inclinable to break up, having first assured me that they should take my company as a favour any Thursday evening, if I came that way. I confess I did not sleep all night with reflecting on what had passed; and could not resolve with myself whether these humorous gentlemen in masquerade were to be ranked with the denomination of knights-errant, or plain robbers. This I must tell you, by the bye, that with respect both to honesty and hardship, their life resembles much that of hussars, since drinking is all their delight, and plundering their employment.

'Before I conclude my epistle, it is fit I should inform you, that they did me the honour (with a design perhaps to have received me into their order) of acquainting me with those rules by which their society was governed. In the first place, the Black Prince assured me, "that the government was perfectly monarchical; and that, when upon expeditions, he had an absolute command; but in the time of peace (continued he), and at the table, government being no longer necessary I condescend to eat and drink familiarly with my subjects as friends.

' "We admit no man into our society, till he has been twice drunk among us, that we may be precisely acquainted with his temper, in compliance with the old proverb: 'Women, children and drunken folks speak truth!' but if the person who sues to be admitted declares solemnly

he was never drunk in his life, and it appears plainly to
the society, in such case this rule is dispensed with, and
the person before admission is only bound to converse
with us a month.

' "As soon as we have determined to admit him, he is
then to equip himself with a good mare or gelding, a brace
of pistols, and a gun of the size of this, to be on the saddle-
bow; then he is sworn upon the horns over the chimney;
and having a new name conferred by the society, is there-
by entered upon the roll, and from that day forward considered as a lawful member. I shall only remark one thing
more, which is, the phrase we make use of in speaking
of one another; viz. 'He is a very honest fellow, and one of
us'; for you must know it is the first article in our creed,
that there's no sin in deer-stealing."

'In the morning, having given my landlady the crown
piece, I found her temper so much altered for the better,
that, in my conscience I believe she was not in the humour
to have refused me anything, no, not even the last favour :
and so walking down the yard and finding my horse in
pretty tolerable order, I speeded directly home, as much
in amazement at the new people I had discovered, as the
Duke of Alva's huntsmen when they found an undiscov-
ered people in Spain by following their master's hawk
over the mountains.'

The passion that the Waltham Blacks had for venison
seems quite peculiar. Perhaps it may partly be accounted
for by the fact that venison was very difficult to buy. The
landowners who owned herds of deer were not inclined
to sell the meat. Then, of course, there was the underlying
idea which was entertained by many members of the
public outside the ranks of professional poachers, that
deer, being a wild animal, could be killed by any man
and that no crime should have been incurred in such hunting. The law thought otherwise and provided the death
penalty for poachers. Moreover, when poachers were convicted they were invariably hanged, publicly of course,
amid scenes of general satisfaction. It does not seem to

have occurred to the authorities to exercise any clemency in their favour, so that the Waltham Blacks were in fact indulging in a deadly game.

What did the Waltham Blacks really have in mind? I think perhaps they were social rebels, early eighteenth-century teddy boys who felt themselves to be outside society and therefore determined to form their own society. As they proudly said it was formed strictly on the monarchical pattern, the king exacting instant obedience from his subjects except when off duty. They seem to have had a crude kind of chivalry and they were a fairly select club because those wishing to join them had to go through a period of probation.

What it was that changed the Waltham Blacks to conceive an assassination we do not know, but we do know that they did hold up the coach from London near Farnham Holt and publicly executed a Mr. Pottinger who was a rich city merchant and lived in the neighbourhood. The assassination of Mr. Pottinger was easy to explain for it was his habit to travel with as much gold on his person as he could carry. I think he was one of those rich men who feel acutely uncomfortable without immediate money available. Be this as it may, the Waltham Blacks laid an ambush for the coach, sprang on Mr. Pottinger, beat him to death and took his money.

Whether or not the Waltham Blacks hoped to buy venison with the money we do not know but presumably as this seems to have been the beginning and end of their ambition, this is what they hoped to do.

Before the assassination of Mr. Pottinger the Waltham Blacks, although they were hanged when they were caught, were not universally hated. They were described as a merry crowd and they were thought of as criminal sportsmen. However, even in 1723 the assassination in broad daylight of a wealthy city merchant stirred the peace-keeping authorities into intense activity and a hunt for the Waltham Blacks was started. Several of them were caught, including John and Edward Pink of Portsmouth, who, before this, had a very good reputation for honesty and hard work but who seemed to have been mad about venison. We can only assume, because these days we cannot relate facts without a psychological explanation, that venison was a symbol to these men and that they were addicted to their symbol. In other words, they were venison perverts. However, the round and ready justice of the early eighteenth century did not bother with any such plausible excuses. Six of the Waltham Blacks, including the two Pinks, were hanged one summer evening in June 1724.

The Waltham Blacks never recovered from the blow. Perhaps the survivors came to the conclusion that the game was not worth the gallows. So the surviving members of the fraternity, having escaped the rope, abandoned their king, the constitution, their regalia, their customs and even their all-consuming passion for deer meat. It seems almost a pity that they should become normal members of the public again, for though we may disapprove of the Waltham Blacks, in principle at any rate, and of their dastardly assassination in practice, yet until they turned to murder they did provide the England of their day with one of its strangest stories, stranger far than fiction and stranger than any story which any writer was likely to invent.

12

Assassination Abominable

POLITICAL assassination is always terrifying, but sometimes it is carried out with a savagery that is revolting. This was the case when on the 17th of July 1958 the entire Royal Family of Iraq were butchered by the men of Brigadier Qasim. Less than ten years later it is almost impossible to believe the facts, so ghastly are they, but it all took place and in order to understand how it was possible that this should happen it is necessary to know something of the background.

Under the Treaty of Lausanne in 1923 the Turks renounced sovereignty over Mesopotamia. The old and great Ottoman Empire was finally breaking up and, as the age of universal independence had not yet come, the colonial powers, Britain and France, which were already on the spot, were moving in.

A provisional Arab government was set up in Mesopotamia in November 1920, and in August 1921 the Emir Faisal, the third son of ex-King Hussein of the Hejaz, was elected King of Iraq.

In 1939 King Faisal II, grandson of Faisal I, acceded to the throne at the age of three on the death of his father, King Ghazi, and until 1953, when Faisal II ascended the throne, Iraq was ruled by Prince Abdulilah as Regent.

It was the young King Faisal, a gentle, intelligent and progressive young man, together with Prince Abdulilah, as well as all the other members of the Royal Family, including baby princesses, who were monstrously murdered in treacherous circumstances at the beginning of Brigadier Qasim's coup. The mob also murdered Prime Minister Nuri-el-Said by splitting his body in two.

This is what happened on the dreadful morning.

Nuri-el-Said had ruled Iraq on behalf of the Crown with a strong hand, believing that the Iraqi people only understood firm power. Prince Abdulilah was generally believed to be the power behind the throne and no one attributed any of the failings of the regime to the young King, who was generally thought to be a kindly and sensible person. However, for many years there had been a history of revolt in Iraq. The government was presented to the people by the revolutionaries as being a 'puppet' of the imperialists. In spite of unparallelled prosperity brought about by the discovery and exploitation of oil the revolutionaries were able to convince some of the townspeople and some units of the army that the government was too much subject to foreign influence. This was the real reason behind the revolution. Another reason was that the people of Iraq never accepted the fiction of democracy, the best but hardest form of government which cannot exist unless the people assume that power lies in the hands of a civil cabinet. As soon as the army discovers that it can take over in a matter of hours democracy is doomed.

The constitution of Iraq was called a constitutional monarchy and it was hereditary in the family of King Faisal. It had a Chamber of Deputies of one hundred and forty-five members, freely elected by adult male suffrage. In the senate not more than a quarter of the total number of deputies was appointed by the King.

General Qasim, a cadaverous, fanatical army officer who seemed to be consumed with hate, was able to impose his will on sufficient of the army to engineer the coup. It was not the fact of a coup itself that shocked the world —but its method.

The revolutionaries had gone into hiding the evening before the coup, keeping in telephonic communication with their units, and at 4 a.m., just before dawn, they struck. They seized the Ministry of War, the police head-quarters and the radio station and at the same time made straight for the palace, still the main seat of power in Iraq.

The royal guards were outnumbered, but as soon as the rebels opened fire the palace guard replied effectively. Fighting continued for over two hours and several men were killed on either side. The King, now surrounded by his entire family, wished to stop the slaughter. Further resistance it was obvious would result in the extermination of his loyal guard. He therefore enquired whether he and his family would be offered a safe conduct out of the country and the reply was that this would be granted.

The family formed into procession led by the King, each of the men holding the Koran and the women having a replica of the Koran on a chain round their neck. This was to ensure immunity, because it was unthinkable that they would be murdered with the Koran in their hand after the promise of safe conduct.

As soon as the King came into sight and the whole family were within range they were mowed down by machine-gun fire from every direction. They all fell bleeding and writhing on the pathway. Soldiers with bayonets then went round finishing off any survivors, including some small princesses who because of their height had escaped the first lethal dose of machine-gun fire. Brigadier Qasim and his troops then entered the Palace and sacked it.

It so happened that shortly after the revolution I had to fly into Baghdad to fulfil a commission for my publisher. From a friend who had been a tutor to the young King I knew something of Baghdad as it had been before the revolution, a delightful city for foreigners who were apt to say that it was the peace and tranquillity that attracted them so much. I had some introductions from the Iraq Embassy to facilitate my mission and I put up at the Iraq Hotel which the week before had been the Regent Palace Hotel. It was not a good hotel but it was the best we could obtain at short notice. We were given an un-appetising little double room. The tariff was out of all proportion to the amenities. It was quite expensive.

I learned to my horror that two Jordanian politicians, one a very old man, the Deputy Premier, Ibrahim Hashim, had been torn to pieces by the crowd at the same time that Suleiman Tonham, the Jordanian Defence Minister, had also been murdered. These officials had been in Baghdad on military duties in connection with the pact of unity between Iraq and Jordan.

That night after dinner we ventured for a moment into the street and saw a military car pass heavily guarded. People were cheering. It was Brigadier Qasim, the new ruler, on his way to a conference. I caught a glimpse of his face, a strong quiet man, cadaverous, with a look of dynamic intensity.

The business which I had undertaken for my publisher did not take very long and through the good offices of Major Salim al-Fakhri, the director of Baghdad Radio, I obtained a ticket to visit the trial of members of the former regime which was taking place. When I arrived the court room was packed. Said Quazzar, the former Minister of Interior, was on trial. He was a handsome man, standing erect in the dock. He was not allowed to sit. The proceedings were a mockery of justice. The president of the court, known as the People's Court, opened the proceedings by saying: 'I am a self-made man. My father was a butcher of sheep. I am a butcher of traitors.' He interrupted the proceedings from time to time to make short revolutionary speeches. He also announced the result of the football match against Czechoslovakia. Later when questioned about these interpolations he replied that they were irrelevancies in the best tradition of the British Bench! But the real terror came from the public in the packed court, for, on a sign from some unseen leader, when there was a lull in proceedings, they would break into a screaming chant denouncing the prisoner and demanding his blood.

In this atmosphere, even as a lawyer, it was not easy to discover what the charges against the former Minister really were, but I managed to extract them. There were three in number. The first charge was that in his official capacity in December 1953 he had ordered police to shoot on strikers in Bosra. The second charge was that he had manipulated elections. The third charge was that he had stirred up tribal revolt to suit his own purposes. He was also charged with being responsible for the torture of detainees in the police department. The *Iraq Times* reporting the matter concluded with these words: 'At the end of his speech the military prosecutor Colonel Mohamed Amin asked the court to cut off the head of the butcher Said Quazzar, the servant of imperialism and its obedient dog.'

Said Quazzar, the prisoner, who acted throughout with great courage, though he was broken in the end by the ghoulish denunciation of the mob, made a statement in which he denied the charges and said that he had always done his best to serve his country and his king. He hinted that those who now tried him might one day find themselves victims of a similar persecution.

It is, I think, impossible to understand the awful incident of Brigadier Qasim's seizure of power without knowing something of the mentality of Qasim and his immediate entourage. In one of the first pamphlets issued by his government after seizing power the real feeling behind the revolution reveals itself. The pamphlet opens in this manner:

'The Iraqi revolution is the culmination of a bitter stubborn and protracted struggle since the days before 1914. It was characterised from the beginning by force and violence. The colonial powers never hesitated to use the vilest means of maintaining their interests and privileges in Iraq, resorting to brute force, terror and subjugation to muffle the voice of the people ...'

A little later even the Crown is implicated:

'The chains closing on the people's neck thus extended

from Imperialism to the treacherous kingship, to ruling cliques of wicked henchmen brought up by imperialism, then to the feudal sheiks. . . .

'The tryrant knew that the people's soul was burning with revenge to break its chains and smash down its enemies.'

This seems to an outsider to be the language of Moscow. There was no real justification for the murders of the leaders of the old regime, certainly none for the killing of the Royal Family. Under Nuri-el-Said, Iraq had been well governed in the sense that great public works had been instituted, the oil industry had been encouraged and extended, irrigation had been enormously increased. It is also fair to say that revolt had been sternly repressed. The revolt of Brigadier Qasim and his brother officers had long been planned. Three times its execution was imminent, but it was postponed because circumstances were not completely right. Colonel Aref had been co-hero with Brigadier Qasim, but Qasim could tolerate no rivals. The government of Qasim was in substance a military government so that far from increasing democratic rights in Iraq the only result was that the freely elected Chamber of Deputies, which had been the most important part of the constitution under the King, was banished overnight.

However, the Qasim regime grew power-crazy and Qasim himself became most peculiar. He had never been a balanced man. On the 8th of February 1963 his regime was overthrown and the following day Quasim was executed. For a time the Ba'ath party retained power, but dissensions in the government followed, jeopardising the national life, and then President Aref took control on November 18th, 1963. So the evil regime of Brigadier Qasim was brought to an end.

It is perhaps interesting to speculate on the different ways in which nations react at the time of a revolution. Certainly the Communist nations, and those who have fallen under Communist influence, seem to be more violent. In the Russian revolution itself the Czar, Czarina and the Czarovitch were murdered much in the same manner as was King Faisal. In Egypt, however, when King Farouk was deposed, he was given three days to pack his treasures on the royal yacht which was permitted to sail to a foreign port, bringing him to safety. In Thailand in 1932 when the one-hundred-and-fifty-year-old absolute rule of the Chakri dynasty was brought to an end the King was treated with much respect and merely asked to sign a constitution, which he did. In Zanzibar the Sultan was lucky to escape to Britain with his life. It all depends on the background and the temper of the people.

Certainly dictators do not seem to fare very well. Mussolini was left swinging by his feet from a rope on a public highway with his mistress swinging beside him.

In Rhodesia, when the government of Ian Smith seized power, the Queen's representative, Sir Humphrey Gibbs, was allowed to remain in Government House. His official cars were taken away from him and the trappings of executive power were, of course, denied him. But no violence of any kind came to his person and at the moment he is still in his official residence, as it were, holding the fort. Perhaps the luckiest ruler to escape assassination was the Emperor Hirohito of Japan, because for four years the government over which he effectively presided had ruled by terror and torture as a deliberate policy. However, the Americans decided that he might be a bulwark against Communism, so, instead of being tried as a war criminal, he was groomed into being a mildly democratic and amiable head of state. This must have been quite a shock for him, but at least it was preferable to an ignominious trial and execution. Incidentally, by his example and the exercise of an enormous prestige he has added greatly not only to the stability of Japan but to her rapid economic recovery.

How did it come about that Brigadier Qasim, who by no means had all the army behind him, was able to carry out his coup? The answer is, of course, that he did it by taking full advantage of the element of surprise. The modern technique of revolution has been to seize power in the early hours of the morning and then to broadcast that one is the new government of the country, although ninety per cent of the country may not even know what has happened. Qasim did exactly this. Nuri-el-Said, who was said to have eyes at the back of his head, was not perhaps as vigilant as he had been in the past. Or perhaps he thought that the rebels would not dare to strike. But I think that a very important factor was the personality of the young King. Although kind and tolerant, he was not the Eastern idea of a ruler. He had not the instantaneous reaction that his cousin King Hussein so notably possesses. Nor had he Hussein's ability to smell treachery. Nor had he Hussein's close link with the actual people of the country, the farmers, the Bedouins. Although both men had been foreign-educated, Hussein remained essentially a man of the desert. He could go back there and fight from there at any moment. King Faisal had not this essential contact. Had Faisal been more ruthless and more alert, taking things into his own hands, he would probably still be ruler of Iraq today.

The assassination of King Faisal seems to us of peculiar horror because of the wanton desecration of the Koran and the treachery with which it was accomplished. There is no other assassination in modern times quite like it. It should teach us a lesson so that we should be in no doubt as to the dark and terrible forces that can be released when revolution comes.

13

Like a Colossus

SHAKESPEARE was a professional writer and commercial playwright and his genius was just a bonus
added to his competence, a happy addition that illuminated and transformed everything he wrote, even his bad
plays. Of course he did not have a research department
working for him, nor is there any evidence that he ever
employed anyone to do his research for him. What he
appears to have done is to have read several accounts of a
great historical incident and torn the guts out of it. He
was not worried about authenticity. What he was worried
about was whether the play would bring in the cash cus-
tomers. He does not appear to have torn up much of
his writing, but he corrected a great deal of it.

His work was nearly always done in a hurry and very
often in the threatre so that actors would come up to
him and say, 'I can't say this line', then Shakespeare would
re-write it so that the written and spoken words could
marry more easily. Shakespeare wrote for a living, not to
achieve fame. Fame was thrust upon him by the verdict
of history. What he really loved was life and for many
years he was so busy indulging in drinking sprees and in
chasing women that he found it very difficult to fit in the
time for writing. Later when he settled down his habits
became less irregular, but, oddly enough, his very greatest plays seem to have been written in his chaotic period.
Certainly his 'final period' contained his weakest plays.

It follows from this that he almost always improved upon history. His account of the assassination of Julius Caesar has burnt itself into the memories of schoolboys everywhere, and so, of course, has Mark Antony's wonderful and moving funeral oration which was really the first speech for the prosecution of the assassins. Nevertheless, what really happened seems to have been somewhat different.

Caesar's own familiar friend in whom he trusted, Decimus Brutus, brother of his bosom companion Marcus Brutus, came to persuade him to come to his murder. Caesar never went guarded or armed and knew no fear. As soon as he was seated in the Senate, Cimber pulled his cloak as a signal, Cassius (not perhaps Caius but another —alter e Cassiis, Sueton) stabbed him from behind and then the rest who had crowded around fell on him. Caesar recognised his fate and with true grandeur made no struggle, but wrapped his toga round him, drawing it over his head, so that he might fall decently, and sank down without a word at the foot of Pompey's statue. Suetonius expressly says so, and mentions only as a tradition that he said to Marcus Brutus in Greek, *Kai su teknon?*' ('And thou too, my son?') The famous '*Et tu Brute*' rests on no sufficient authority.

The fortunes of the conspirators and the ruin of the republic, which, after Caesar's death, sank for centuries into a military despotism, is now well known and with minor differences most students are agreed on the major developments. Antony's speech at Caesar's funeral, though not in Shakespeare's words, is an historical fact and brought about the ruin of the guilty men who had destroyed the great Roman captain.

It is impossible to pass by the testimony of the two greatest poets who have lived since Caesar on the guilt of his assassins. Shakespeare's indictment of them is overwhelming and convincing, and it is interesting that Dante, in the lowest hell of his *Inferno*, places the three archtraitors of the world, whom the three-headed Lucifer crunches in his triple jaws, as Judas Iscariot, Brutus, and Cassius.

This suggests a very curious parallel between the traitor of Jesus and the traitor of Caesar, namely the murder by treachery on a false accusation of aiming at kingship, this taking place after a last supper where the conversation turns on death. What kind of man was Julius Caesar in terms of today? He seems to come through the two thousand years of history not only as a great man but as a man with a shining character. His personal accomplishments and courage, his talents for war, his magnaminity, and his capacity for civil affairs, render him perhaps the most remarkable man of any age. He has been compared to Napoleon, but Napoleon often had a brutal disregard for the health and lives of his soldiers. Caesar, by all accounts, was a man of constant compassion and this was in an age when compassion and humanitarian feelings in general were hardly recognised as a virtue.

One writer says of Caesar quite justly that he was 'at one and the same time a general, a statesman, a law-giver, a jurist, an orator, a poet, an historian, a philosopher, a mathematician and an architect'. He was equally fitted to excel in all these manifold activities and indeed when he did apply his mind and energy to any one subject he did excel in it. As a writer and an orator he received the highest praise from Cicero, and his *Commentaries*, written in a plain, attractive style, are a model of their kind. He wrote three books on the *Civil Wars* and his name appeared on books on the Alexandrine, African and Spanish wars respectively, but these were probably written by Hirtius, who seems to have been his 'ghost'. Unfortunately, but very naturally, some of his best works are lost to us for ever; for instance, we do not have his poems, his work in the Latin language, or his biographical sketch, the *Anti-Cato*, and we have also lost his *Auguries*. All these were praised by his contemporaries. His *Commentaries* have passed through numberless editions. Perhaps the best is still the one published in Stuttgart in 1822.

So we have here all the ingredients of assassination at its most dramatic and in its most horrific form. The victim is a man without peers in his own time, a figure who did indeed stride the world. The assassins were his friends or veiled enemies. The murder took place in the most public place in Rome and there is no doubt that the conspirators intended to tell the people that they had rid Rome of a tyranny. To substantiate this allegation it was necessary to persuade the people that Caesar was determined to become not only King of Rome but a creature divine here on earth.

When Ceasar returned to Rome for the last time he could justly celebrate a quadruple triumph, for he had achieved victories in Gaul, Egypt, Pontus and Africa. At this time victory and vengeance were practically synonymous terms, and we read with astonishment of the clemency of Caesar. No difference was made between aristocrats and democrats; those who had borne arms against him he freely forgave, on the sole condition of the restoration of order. When these orders were issued the public of the defeated nation could hardly believe them. It was feared that they were a trick, but as soon as it began to be felt that this was not a mask for some ulterior design, the greatest joy prevailed. Nothing was too good for such a hero. He was made a dictator for ten years with power to nominate consuls, a new and more stringent censorship, under the title of Prefect of Public Morals, was created for him, so that he might cope with the sink of patrician dissolute luxury.

Caesar had but one more campaign to carry through and he started from Rome in a carriage, in mid-winter, for Spain, where the sons of Pompey had raised a dangerous force. During the greater part of the year he was absent in Spain. He won the great battle of Munda in which thirty thousand men are said to have fallen on Pompey's side. Caesar remained until the autumn, ensuring the pacification of Spain and order for the years that lay ahead.

These campaigns were but the termination of a life devoted to the Roman cause. Julius Caesar was certainly born with a golden spoon. He was the son of Julius Caesar and Aurelia. His aunt Julia was the wife of Caius Marius. He had therefore as uncle Sextus Julius Caesar the Consul and Marius, already no less than six times Consul. At the age of fourteen Julius was made *flamen dialis* or priest of Jupiter and a member of the sacred college of Augurs, with a handsome income.

Caesar is described at this time as 'a tall slight handsome youth with dark piercing eyes, a sallow complexion, large nose, full lips, features refined and intellectual, neck sinewy and thick beyond what might have been expected from the generally slender figure'. His first two marriages were arranged for him.

While still a youth Julius Caesar was captured by pirates and held to ransom for a huge sum—ten thousand pounds in Roman money—in Rhodes. It is typical of Caesar that he made the best of his confinement, joining in the sports and games of the pirates, but at the same time warning them with quiet detachment that they would suffer for their sins. He was as good as his word, for after the ransom had been paid and Caesar was free again he immediately seized some armed vessels and took them back to capture all the pirates whom he took to Pergamus. They were given a meticulous trial but were all convicted and all executed. Julius Caesar was not a youth to be trifled with.

The extraordinary story of Caesar's career abroad and in Rome has all the drama of high politics. Perhaps Pompey was the greatest enemy Caesar ever had. Pompey recognised Caesar's greatness immediately and hated him. Pompey drew his strength from the aristocrats of Rome and from the wealthy. Caesar was the hero of the people and as Caesar had unmatched eloquence it was always a danger dreaded by Pompey that Caesar might be allowed to address the multitude. In their last confrontation Caesar acted with his usual lightning speed, crossing the little

Rubicon, and descending on Rome. Even now he paused at Arininum to offer to lay down his arms if Pompey would do the same. An evasive answer was returned and Caesar marched on Rome. Pompey's supporters fled to him and Rome greeted Caesar as its hero once more, but Pompey sailed for Greece and became a threat in exile to Caesar.

The most astounding part of the long history of Caesar's service is the way he was able to divide his activities between planning elaborate campaigns on the grandest scale, organising administration over large areas at the highest level, and setting up the mechanics of a police force to maintain order. At the same time he was able to return to Rome to renew his contacts with the people of the great city from whom he derived his power.

On his return to Rome for the last time the welcome to Caesar surpassed all previous welcomes. It was now clear that all roads led to Rome. Rome was the capital of the world. The Roman Empire stretched as far north as Britain, as far west as Morocco and as far east as the Persian Gulf. It was a fabulous achievement and within its confines there reigned peace and a sophisticated culture that put to shame the barbarians outside the imperial precincts. The people of Rome recognised this with a glowing pride and they wished to heap honours on the man who, more than anyone else, had achieved the miracle of Roman supremacy. His portrait was ordered to be on all coins; the month Quintilis was renamed Julius. He was named the Liberator and further was created Consul for ten years and Imperator for life—giving him the military power of life and death except in Rome. The word imperator implied commander-in-chief. It did not imply the kingship, which, of course, was designated Rex.

The whole Senate took an oath to watch over his life; Cicero was among the most abject on this score. Caesar seems to have paid little heed to flattery, but went on with his plans for consolidating the great Roman dominions.

He cut short the corn grants which kept numbers in idle readiness for revolt; he filled up the ranks of a greatly enlarged Senate with Gauls, with provincials, even with representatives of freed men, poor folk who had once been slaves and by merit or the generosity of their masters had recovered freedom. The aristocracy were aghast. Caesar forbade the absurdly costly banquets, the sedan-chairs, the licentiousness of the gilded youth of the day. He began with the help of the Varro to instal public libraries in large towns and made elaborate plans for draining the Pontine marshes. He was a great planner and aimed at cutting a better channel for the Tiber and for cutting the isthmus of Corinth. He found time to start on a digest of all Roman Law. All this he was attempting to accomplish in the few months after his last return. He was resisting the adulation and applause of interested parties, but he could not entirely stop it. The Senate ordered his statue to be placed in all temples, in the rostra, and on the Capitol itself, an eighth after the seven kings of Rome.

Finally they formally pronounced him not man at all, but a god, Divus Julius; a temple was order to be built and Mark Antony was named its priest. But Caesar knew well that some of the flatterers were longing for his death. He detected the snare of the offer from the Senate to crown him King of Rome and bluntly refused.

When the mob saluted him by the new title he replied: 'I am not King, but Caesar.' On the 15th of February at the festival of Lupercalia Antony formally offered to place a regal tiara on Caesar's head. Caesar answered in a clear loud voice: 'Romans have no king but God,' and he ordered it to be placed on the head of the statue of Jupiter. An inscription on brass recorded the fact that the crown had been offered by the people and refused by Caesar.

This, in brief, was the background to one of the world's most astounding assassinations. The conspirators knew that they were running an awful risk, for it was always possible that the Roman mob, if they heard that Caesar had been murdered, might seek out and crucify his killers, but the conspirators were confident that they could manipulate the mob. They did not anticipate the speech of Mark Antony.

In writing of Julius Caesar and the men who assassinated him one has in the end to fall back on the genius of Shakespeare. *Julius Caesar* was published in the First Folio of 1623, having been written in 1599, and there is a record in the diary of a German named Platter that he actually saw the play acted on the 21st of September of that year. Shakespeare has almost certainly got his Caesar wrong. At this time Caesar was not a man of failing power, nor was he superstitious and pompous, but it may well be that Shakespeare drew him thus to accentuate the drama, or even to fit the part for some actor he had in mind to play Caesar. *Julius Caesar* is an astounding play and reads or acts today as freshly as it did four hundred years ago. The menace of the Ides of March are as threatening now as they were then. The critics claim that *Julius Caesar*, being the first of the tragedies that Shakespeare wrote in his early maturity, marks the beginning of the psychological treatment that he later perfected. However this may be, it is a play without comparison. The craft and the cunning and the superb rhetoric of Antony's farewell to Caesar could be taken today as a model for an advocate who aimed at clarity and persuasion.

> 'Here, under leave of Brutus, and the rest
> Come I to speak in Caesar's funeral.
> He was my friend, faithful and just to me;
> But Brutus says, he was ambitious;
> And Brutus is an honourable man.
> He hath brought many captives home to Rome,
> Whose ransoms did the general coffers fill;
> Did this in Caesar seem ambitious?
> When that the poor have cried, Caesar hath wept;
> Ambition should be made of sterner stuff.'

In spite of their familiarity the words ring out as clearly

as ever they did and Antony's last eulogy of his friend stands for all time, irresistible and sublime:

> 'This was the noblest Roman of them all;
> All the conspirators, save only he
> Did that they did in envy of great Caesar;
> He only, in a general honest thought,
> And common good to all, made one of them.
> His life was gentle; and the elements
> So mix'd in him that nature might stand up,
> And say to all the world, "This was a man!" '

The great assassins and the great assassinations will always be with us, but it is doubtful whether ever again so poignant a tragedy as the assassination of Julius Caesar will be enacted. Even today ordinary people can learn something from the envy and treachery of the assassins of Caesar and from the manifold gifts and magnanimity of the man they murdered.

14

Assassination Wholesale

C OMPARISONS are often made between the British system of justice and Continental systems, sometimes to
the detriment of the latter. We like our rules which govern
the arrest, the caution and the interrogation of prisoners
because we feel that these Judges Rules, as they are called,
protect possibly innocent people when suddenly confronted with a desperate situation.

In countries that have based their law on the Code
Napoleon quite a different view is taken. It is thought that
logically every innocent citizen should be able to establish
the fact that he has not been connected with a particular
crime. No doubt, in nine cases out of ten, innocent people
can do this, often by referring back to diaries, office calen-
dars or worksheets which may prove that at the critical
time they were somewhere else. Nevertheless, until a few
months ago we prided ourselves on the restrictions we
placed on police interrogation and it is only very recently
that, to my mind, a misguided effort has been made by
certain judicial gentlemen to weigh the scales more heavily
against the suspect.

Another characteristic of English law in which we
rightly take pride is the comparative speed of English justice and in this respect we compare favourably not only
with the Continental system but with the American system as well, which, though basically founding its laws and
procedures on the old British pattern, has introduced such

a complex of appeals and injunctions and reprieves that it is possible for quite simple criminal cases to hang about undecided for years.

Both these points I have made—the protection of the suspect after arrest and under interrogation and the speed of criminal justice—were highly important when on the 16th of April 1956 John Gilbert Graham of Denver, U.S.A., was indicted for the murder of forty-four persons, passengers on an aeroplane, though the District Attorney only proceeded with the charge of murdering his mother, Mrs. Daisy King, by planting a time-bomb in the airliner D.C.-6B at Denver airport on Tuesday the 1st of November 1955, Mrs. King being one of the passengers on that plane.

The prosecution opened their case on the 16th of April 1956. The verdict was not given until the 4th of May.

The case against Graham was founded on a confession he was said to have made to the investigating authorities. Before making this statement he was not warned, as he would have been in Britain, that he was not bound to say anything but that, if he did, it would be taken down and might be used in evidence. He was subjected to seven hours of third-degree 'grilling'. The police were assured that they had got their man and they had no intention of allowing him to escape the full penalty of his atrocious crime.

Graham's arrest followed weeks of the most laborious and painstaking research, including a truly wonderful reconstruction of the plane for which no praise can be too high. Everybody connected with the case was up to their eyes in detail. What does not appear to have happened, at least during the first week, was for the investigating team to attempt a clear, unhurried assessment of the evidence and the probabilities it gave rise to.

No one sat down, at once, to reason along these lines.

This plane disaster was caused either by accident or design. If it was an accident it is entirely a matter for the experts to say how it happened, and what lesson could be learnt from it. A commission might apportion blame if indeed anyone was to blame. No question of criminal liability arose and the utmost deliberation in pursuing the matter would achieve the best results in the public interest.

If the disaster had been caused by design this was murder, and murder on a scale hardly conceived before. The murder of the passengers could only have been caused by a time-bomb and the only place such a bomb could have been planted in the plane—unless the mechanism was of unusual complexity—was Denver. Who then stood to benefit by the death of the Denver passengers? This line of reasoning would have brought the authorities to John Gilbert Graham much more swiftly than the methods that were pursued. We must, however, pay tribute to the great amount of zealous work that was in fact done to achieve the same result.

What were the facts known to the authorities on the 1st of November, the fatal Tuesday?

They knew that the airliner D.C.-6B, in charge of a Captain Hall, had come into Stapleton Airport at Denver from New York and Chicago, Denver being one of its scheduled stops. Four new passengers, all of them women, boarded the plane at Denver. The plane had taken off nearly half an hour late, and ten minutes later it had crashed in flames in Weld County, some forty miles away.

The day was clear, with no snow, ice, or fog, and Captain Hall had radioed the airport after take-off that all was well. Immediately before the explosion witnesses described the airliner as flying at fifteen hundred feet. It should have been at an altitude of at least six thousand, a fact never explained.

It was not until a week after the disaster that the Federal Bureau of Investigation, in the person of Roy K. Moore, was brought into the affair. From that point the investigation took a new degree of cogency and uniformity.

The investigators examining the damage, both the main body of the plane and the remnants that were scattered over a five-mile stretch of country, were able to give a mass of detailed information from which these salient facts emerged. Two explosions had occurred. All the witnesses were agreed on this. One, the first, had been while the plane was in flight, the second occurred just before the plane hit the ground. The reconstruction experts were able to say that one luggage compartment, underneath the passenger accommodation, had been exploded with a force that could not be accounted for by any possible ignition of the oils or chemicals that the airliner carried for its own propulsion. The force of the blast had been immense, the kind of force only procured by an explosive in large quantity. Once these facts became known the probing of the Denver women passengers became the focal point of the case.

It was reasonably certain that the time-bomb, if time-bomb it was, must have been planted in Denver. Such contraptions, if made by amateur electricians, have a very limited delayed action, nor is the delay always accurate! True, the explosion had occurred only ten minutes after take-off, but the plane had been half an hour late. The murderer could not have anticipated this. Had the plane been reasonably on time the murderer would have planted his device in good time and the airliner, at the time of the explosion, would have been flying very high over the Rocky Mountains. If this had happened recovery of the debris would have been very much more difficult and the crime of John Gilbert Graham might never have been brought home to him.

When the F.B.I. had finally decided that Denver was the place where this crime had been conceived and executed they were well on the way to their quarry. Who stood to gain by the death of one of the four ladies who had boarded the plane at Stapleton Airport?

A number of red herrings were patiently pursued before being discarded. A recent trade-union dispute in the airline industry was thought to be a circumstance requiring investigation. The possibility that the disaster had been caused by a lunatic led to a patient check of these unfortunates, and of weak-minded persons who had been at liberty at the time of the crash. Both lines of enquiry were quite fruitless. Moore and his colleagues settled down to screen the Denver passengers.

From this point it did not take them long to light on Mrs. Daisy King, a victim, and her son, by a former marriage, John Gilbert Graham, a hulking young man of twenty-three, over six feet in height, with thick black hair that came very low on his forehead, whose features seemed to wear a perpetual puzzled scowl. True, Mr. Graham's family was entirely respectable. His mother, who had boarded the airliner to visit a sister, was quite well off. His wife, Marion, a year younger than her husband, was a girl of exemplary character, and the couple had two children, Allan, who was two, and Susan, who had not yet celebrated her first birthday.

But the record of Graham himself was sinister and significant.

He had held jobs in Alaska and Colorado in lumbering and construction work, in the course of which he might well have picked up a working knowledge of explosives. He had a criminal record of theft, forgery and bootlegging, and, most remarkable of all, when a theft had occurred at the restaurant he ran jointly with his mother an explosion had occurred which had apparently destroyed the evidence of the crime. The investigating police were at once convinced that here was their man and from this point onwards they assumed the guilt of their quarry.

Let me say at this point that the American public and Press reacted in an entirely different way when these facts were made known to the way British public opinion would have reacted. Although in both countries the horror and disgust would have been widespread and sincere, in Britain, we may be sure, the question of Graham's mental state would have been the subject of heated and learned discussion in the columns of the newspapers. The line of argument 'This is the act of a madman, therefore Graham must be insane' would have been strenuously advanced. Petitions would have been signed by well-meaning persons to ensure that the death penalty, on conviction, would not be carried out. The Home Secretary would have been the target of a sickly campaign to save Graham from his fate.

American public opinion seems to have taken the far healthier line: 'If this man did it, the sooner he dies the better.'

From the point at which the police, under the able direction of Mr. Moore, lighted on John Graham, that unsavoury young man seems to have made quite certain, by his own statements, that his fate would be the electric chair.

I find his statements too good to be true, but the record shows that when first questioned by Moore as a suspect he was asked if he knew why his mother's luggage had been overweight. Marion, his wife, had said something about a Christmas present being included in her baggage.

Graham is said to have replied: 'When my mother wasn't looking I stuck in something to surprise her. It was a Christmas present—a seashell kit. She likes that kind of work.'

When Graham said these words it is clear he was taken by surprise, and it may well be that taking a witness by surprise is more likely to evoke a truthful response than warning them of the consequences their answer is likely to have. The dangers, of course, are obvious.

The statement that Graham made at the end of his investigation seems to be divisible into two parts. I find quite credible his description of what happened at the airport. These were his words:

'After my mother had finished checking her baggage my wife and I went with her to the passengers' gate where we bade my mother goodbye and watched her board the plane with the other passengers. We were there for about an hour, and as we were leaving I heard the cashier say that there had been a wreck of an airplane about forty miles out of Denver. Later on that evening, after my wife and I had returned home, we heard over the radio that all the passengers on the plane had been killed.

But, in addition, the authorities produced a detailed confession of the crime, and of the method Graham had employed in making the bomb. He had used twenty-five sticks of dynamite, he had contrived a timing device for an hour and a half. He had used a six-volt battery, and over eight feet of wire to connect the explosive with the detonator. This seems to me quite incredible. If Graham were not a lunatic he must have known that a confession of this detailed kind would seal his fate. Never in a very long experience of criminal capital cases have I known a cunning and capable killer utter the evidence that the authorities are looking for and are unable to supply themselves.

Imagine how different Graham's position would have been had he been charged in Britain. True, he had insured his mother's life on the automatic insurance machine at the airport, but other passengers were insured for greater amounts, and he had not even troubled to ask his mother to sign the insurance slip which, if he were a deliberate murderer, he must have known was necessary to recover the proceeds in the event of death. True, the possession of dynamite could be traced to him, but he had at his disposal several explanations of this that he might have used. With regard to the battery and wires there was no purchase. They were presumably in his possession. If Graham had said nothing, as he would have been advised to do in this country, merely stating that he had no connection whatever with the atrocious crime, it would have been extremely difficult to bring the charge home to him with that degree of certainty that an English court requires. In that case one of the vilest murderers of the century might well have gone unpunished.

There had been precedents for Graham's crime, though in both cases the number of passengers killed was not so

large as in the Denver case. In 1949 three persons had
been convicted in Canada of planting a bomb in a civil airliner to collect insurance, killing the twenty passengers,
one of whom was married to one of the accused. It was
noteworthy that this accused had a double motive. He
got rid of a wife he did not want and was in a position to
claim the insurance money by virtue of the same act. In
the same year there had also been a case of sabotage in the
Philippines, but in that case the death of one or more of
the passengers, rather than the collection of insurance
payments, was the guiding motive.

There were elements of drama in the Graham case
that neither of these cases possessed. The chief ingredient
in the dramatic picture was represented by the delay in the
departure of the airliner. Mrs. King, Graham's mother,
lived at 2650 West Mississippi Avenue, Denver. She could
be relied upon to leave for the airport not more than an
hour before the plane's departure. If she did this, and if
the plane left punctually, there was comfortable time for
John Graham to plant his bomb which would explode
approximately half an hour after take-off.

As we have seen, Graham, with his family, accompanied Mrs. King to the airport. During the half-hour's
delay he must have suffered absolute agony. If the liner
had been delayed another fifteen minutes the explosion
would have taken place on the runway in front of the
buffet where John and his family were sitting sipping
coffee and cakes. According to the evidence John Graham
did not seem unduly perturbed during this time.

After the plane's take-off the family stayed on in the
reception lounge taking their snack. The news of the
disaster reached them there.

A curious point arises. If Graham was serious when he
spent a dollar and a half on insuring his mother's life
why did he not get her to sign the insurance slip, or, if he
thought this would arouse her suspicion, which was most
improbable, why did he not forge her signature? He had
forged signatures before on stolen cheques. The answer

must be that he could hardly do this without his wife knowing and at all costs he must keep his vile design from her.

Yet the chief interest in this extraordinary case must remain the confession, how it came about that, in a charge most difficult to prove, the accused himself should supply the authorities with the very evidence they were looking for, almost in the language they would have chosen.

The confession, if freely given, can only be explained by the remorse of the prisoner. And remorse is not a quality which, as a rule, one finds in murderers of this type. Usually an overwhelming conceit and self-confidence is more typical of the calculating, cold murderer. This is certainly true of the poisoners of whom it is thought that not more than one in four are even charged. It should be equally true of a crime as deliberate in its conception, and cunning in its execution, as John Graham's crime. He started the careful, intricate work on his murderous contraption ten days before he intended to use it. He knew that if he were successful all the passengers and crew, as well as his mother, must perish. He knew that if he was discovered his wife and children must suffer very great shame. Yet he pursues his project to the very end. Then, suddenly, he changes character. Instead of stoutly denying the charge and protesting his innocence to the end, he turns round and supplies the vital confession that assures his own death.

Future students of this truly awful case will, I think, find in the unique and improbable behaviour of John Gilbert Graham, the accused, the chief interest, and the chief puzzle that the case presents.

Whatever the explanation, there can be little doubt that Graham was the culprit, and we need shed no tears over his own fate.

When the jury brought in the verdict of first-degree murder it was felt that a monster had been justly sentenced. And when John Graham was electrocuted public opinion held that the only possible end to the story had come with his instant death.

It is difficult, if one accepts the guilt of John Graham, because of the enormity of his crime, to take a detached view about the more disturbing factors in this case. Matricide, even in these days of easier morals, is regarded as such an awful crime that when one is confronted by it one is apt to be swayed by emotion rather than reason. The fact remains that Graham's confession still seems to be too good to be true, his carelessness and his callousness still appear to be improbable and puzzling, and of course there are those who, while admitting that he was a monster, will say that he was a mad monster, a subject for the psychiatrist, not for the electric chair. No sane man, the argument runs, could have committed this truly abominable crime. I think the answer is that no normal man could have committed it, but John Graham was far from normal. However, I do not doubt that by the laws governing legal insanity in America and in England he was quite sane. What a modern psychiatrist in a modern rehabilitation clinic would make of him I shudder to think.

Experts said that he was a first-class electrical engineer.

15

A Whisper in the Palace

THE story of Siam for the last six hundred years has been the story of the Siamese monarchy which was absolute until the 24th of June 1932, when it became 'constitutional' in the Siamese sense: that is to say the throne retained its immense social prestige, while power was exercised, under the King, largely by a group of army officers.

At the end of the seventeenth and beginning of the eighteenth centuries the capital of Siam was not at Bangkok, the abode of the angels, as it is now, but at Ayuthia, some fifty miles up the Menam river from the sea.

Ayuthia was a fine and resplendent capital city dominated by over fifty temples, each one housing its Buddha or collection of Buddhas. The roofs of the temples gleamed in the Siamese sunshine, luminous and varied, with colours of gold and crimson, green and blue, so that a traveller catching his first sight of the capital might be excused for thinking that this was indeed a paradise on earth. The spires of the temples shot up towards clear blue skies and thousands of priests, in their saffron-coloured robes, roamed the city in the early morning, receiving tributes and food from the populace.

The King of Siam at this time, Phra Narai, the Lord of Life, the reincarnation of Buddha and the supreme King of Siam and her Dependencies, lived in his palace slightly raised above the rest of the city. In the huge royal compound over a hundred elephants were tethered. These were the working elephants of the King. In addition to the working elephants Phra Narai owned seven white elephants—one more than the King of Burma—and no doubt the glory that surrounded him and the good fortune that had blessed his reign was due in no small measure to these white elephants, which were regarded by the devout Siamese as being themselves reincarnations of Buddha, but, of course, at a lower level than a human reincarnation. The work of the city that was not done by the elephants was carried out by the buffaloes, of which there were a great number. It seemed as if each buffalo had a small boy riding on its back who was both its master, its keeper and its friend.

There was not a great deal of industry in the city, as we understand industry, but there was some beautiful workmanship carried out. Vases, urns and other vessels were made very skilfully and in their manufacture gold was embossed on silver in a manner somewhat similar to that employed by the Russians under the Czars. There was quite an industry in weaving cloth—especially silk—and in making glass and pottery, as well as some porcelain, and there was even tin-smelting and gold-beating. But, of course, the kingdom of Siam was an agricultural kingdom and the great river that ran through Ayuthia plastered its rich mud over the valley so that rice grew easily and it was rice with fish that formed the diet of the people. The rivers and lakes swarmed with fish and, as the sun was always shining and the climate was hardly ever unbearably hot, the life of the Siamese was a pleasant life and they formed the opinion that their country was the most desirable nation on earth. In some ways perhaps it was. The Siamese then as now had a good conceit of themselves and the maps that were used at the court of Phra Narai showed Siam as a very large country painted entirely in green and gold, whereas lesser countries like Burma appeared to be quite small and were coloured a rather unattractive dark brown. There was, of course, rivalry between the court of the King of Siam and the court of the King of Ava. It was said that in the remote past the King of Siam had paid a nominal tribute of some golden fruit to the Emperor of China, but this was no longer mentioned at the time we are speaking of. Phra Narai was the unfettered Lord of Siam, as his edicts said, in every direction.

When I say that Phra Narai was an absolute monarch I mean that he was absolute in the old sense, not merely that he had dictatorial powers. He owned all the land of Siam personally and he could give it to whom he chose. He owned all the houses in Siam and all the gold and silver and, of course, all the elephants and all his palaces. His word was law as soon as he had spoken it. Everything he said was taken down by the royal scribes who crouched at the feet of the King. In this way every utterance of the King became automatically the law of Siam.

The King also had the power of life and death and his subjects revered him by demonstrating respect, and indeed awe, in the most extravagant manner. Everyone approached the King kneeling, but this practice was not confined to the monarch but was customary for all inferiors approaching their superiors. Thus a son would kneel in the presence of his father and a grandson, of course, would kneel in the presence of practically everyone. The salutation of the Siamese, which was called the *wai* in the Siamese language, was affected by bringing the hands together palm to palm to the forehead, but there was a refinement of this, the higher the rank of the person saluted the higher the hands were raised, so that when his courtiers were saluting Phra Narai they were kneeling and raising their hands palm to palm high above their heads. They could only look up if he indicated that this was his wish. The body of the King was sacrosanct and it was a capital offence to touch him, so it goes without saying that the King did not shake hands with anyone. Such an idea would have seemed to him quite fantastic.

In fact Phra Narai was an unusual king in Siam.

Although, largely as a matter of prestige, he had a fairly large harem, he only lived habitually with one queen, usually taking a young princess chosen by the Queen to avoid boredom. He was, of course, as devout a Buddhist as any of his subjects and quite a lot of his time was taken up with religious or quasi-religious duties. At the great Buddhist festivals he would proceed to the temple where he would have to listen to the interminable eulogies of the priests and their endless incantations. He was assidious in preserving all the Siamese ceremonies, the ceremony of sowing the seed, which was the ceremony of life itself, the ceremony of the swing, which was a kind of Maundy, for the contestants would swing higher and higher and higher so that one could see their bodies silhouetted against the azure sky, until at last they were able to seize the little bags of royal gold coins in their teeth. Then, of course, there was the ceremony of the departed spirits, when thousands of little paper boats were made, each bearing a candle or candles, which were sent out in the evening on the waters of Menam, so that the whole river danced with light as the tiny craft bobbed and weaved their way towards the sea.

Phra Narai was not at all adverse to the traditional recreations of Siamese royalty. He would sometimes spend a day in his harem, but more often he would go and see the wild elephants surrounded and brought in to be tamed, or he would go and see a cock-fight, or watch his fighting fish, which had a curious grey-green colour until they were angered in the fight, when they turned to scarlet. In April and May the winds were favourable for the sport the Siamese loved best of all, which was kite-flying. It was a complicated business, for it involved a contest in which the victorious kite, by the dint of much strategy and tactics, would swoop on the vanquished kite and bring it down to earth. Needless to say, the royal kite of Phra Narai was the most splendid kite in Siam, purple and red and gold, it roamed the heavens like a kite of God. No one could fly a kite to vanquish the King's kite, for that would have been treason and the penalty for treason in Siam was torture and death, not only for the offending traitor but for all his family as well.

All the evidence we have about Phra Narai seems to suggest that he was cultured and kindly and extremely intelligent. It was, perhaps, his intelligence that prompted him to enquire whether the age-old isolation of Siam could go on for ever. Was it possible to ignore the world at large completely and absolutely? In Ayuthia, seated on his throne in his palace, surrounded by his genuflecting courtiers, listening to the propitious forecasts of the court astrologer, constantly hearing the adulation of his Ministers, it might well have seemed to Phra Narai that his golden world was safe and secure and would never end. The foreigners who came to Ayuthia always came as supplicants usually wishing to trade. They depended entirely on the goodwill of the King. In 1511 the Portuguese had established some intercourse with Siam. Later in the sixteenth century the despicable King of Burma had conquered Siam for a while, but his army had been thrown out before the end of the century and Siamese independence restored.

In 1612 the first English vessel reached Ayuthia, but no commercial relations had been established and this was due in no small measure to the Siamese system of taxation, which was somewhat arbitrary, depending to a large extent on the needs of the Minister who had charge of the state's dealings with foreign merchants. Foreigners did not seem to present any real threat to Siam and it was possible for a Siamese king to draw around himself a gold and exclusive curtain.

Phra Narai had, however, an extraordinary Prime Minister. This gentleman, who, of course, had a Siamese title, was not a Siamese at all but a Greek, Constantine Phaulkon. Phaulkon was a man of immense ability and industry. He had come to Siam, as people did at this time, as an adventurer. He had married a Siamese who belonged to one of the court families and soon spoke

Siamese fluently, both the high language that was used by
the Ministers addressing the King and the low language
which was used in the great market place. He was a man
of commanding presence, with eyes that seemed to penetrate all pretence and to sum up people very quickly.
Phaulkon adopted Siamese dress and when he was able
to render a small service to the Minister of the army—
the *Kalahom*—this great man brought him to the notice
of the King who allowed him to enter the royal service
and wear the royal panung.

The rise of Phaulkon to fame and power was one of the
most romantic stories to come out of South-East Asia. He
rose rapidly in the involved hierarchy of the Palace, serving the King in a variety of ways. Neither the princes who
were nearest to the monarch nor the officials who were
carefully graduated according to their rank could com-
pete with him. He was a marvellous man at getting
things done and it was this quality that appealed to Phra
Narai. Of course, if the King gave an order in Siam
everybody would immediately assent. There would never
be any dispute or objection, but this did not mean that
the King's orders were invariably carried out efficiently.
It was because of this that the King noticed that when a
matter was handled by the Greek Phaulkon it was invariably done speedily and well. Phaulkon showed the King
as much respect as any of his Ministers, but if the King
asked him for an opinion he would not reply, as the Ministers were apt to do, by saying that the King's wish was
their wish. He would give his opinion, couched, of course,
in terms of flattering deference, but it was an opinion
nevertheless. The King did not have to accept it and could
immediately overrule Phaulkon as he could overrule
everyone else, but Phaulkon's advice was often so shrewd,
especially in matters relating to foreigners, that the King
was often impressed and was inclined to take his advice.

So it was that Constantine Phaulkon, who had been a
clerk in a shipping office in Athens, rose to be the greatest
man in Siam, apart from the King. He built himself a

magnificent palace, close to the King's palace in Ayuthia, and foreigners visiting Siam soon discovered that unless they had the ear of Phaulkon nothing could be achieved. Every day at Phaulkon's palace the crowd of petitioners would gather, hoping to be admitted to his presence— men who wanted to mine tin, men who sought a concession to work the sapphire ore of the north-west, men who brought cargoes from Europe and wished to take in exchange cargoes from Siam. It was impossible to see the King. He was surrounded by a protocol so strict that only visiting royalty, and occasionally ambassadors, could hope to be received by him. Phaulkon, on the other hand, could be seen, though it was very difficult. If only one could reach him he was a man capable of giving a quick, decisive and emphatic decision. Because this was the situation the whole business of the state of Siam tended to revolve round the figure of Constantine Phaulkon.

The King of Siam was wont to consult his Ministers at night. This was a very old custom and probably had its origin in secrecy and security. After a meeting of his cabinet Phra Narai would often be left alone with Phaulkon and it was then that the most important words were spoken. From time to time vexatious problems arose and one of them occurred after Phra Narai had been on the throne some years.

In a nutshell the question was: What shall we do about the French? Now the French had turned up in Siam and had sent two or three missions to Ayuthia. This was not important in itself, for, as usual with foreigners, they had come to beg for favour from the King. Now, however, some French troops had come to Paknam at the mouth of the river and there was some talk that the French were intending to build a fort at that place. The King, who in the first instance had welcomed the French, because he thought he might use them as a counter-balance to certain palace intrigues which he had heard about, became somewhat alarmed when he heard what they were up to, for, of course, it was unthinkable that foreign mercenaries should erect fortresses in the domain of the Lord of Life. He consulted Phaulkon and Phaulkon gave some surprising advice. The tenor of his words to the King were as follows:

'As my Supreme Lord is good enough to deign to ask my opinion in the important matter of the foreign French, who have been permitted to come into my Lord's kingdom, may I humbly suggest that we proceed in this matter with the utmost caution? It is well known that His Majesty King Louis XIV of France is a powerful potentate and would like to conclude a treaty with His Majesty the King of Siam. I see no reason to object to this. If we have the French as our friends they will be our powerful allies and other aspiring foreigners, such as the British, who it is said are a waxing race, will be more careful in their dealings with us. I suggest that Your Majesty treats the visiting French with hospitality and at the same time I will send spies to Paknam to see that they do not exceed the bounds of decency. While this is going on I think it would be prudent to send a mission, led by one of Your Majesty's most trusted advisers, to the court of King Louis with some presents for that monarch, who will, of course, send presents to your Siamese Majesty in return. This will open our eyes and enable us to see what the French designs are and your mission will report back the manner of man this monarch is and who his most trusted servants are. They will also report on his army, his navy and his civil service. Moreover, the local French commander in Paknam, knowing that Your Majesty is treating on equal terms with his French Majesty, will be very careful indeed what he does in Siam, for I am quite sure that the decisions made by the French in this part of Asia are not made by local commanders but are made by the French King and his Ministers in Paris or at Versailles. Moreover, Your Majesty, it might be as well, as your mission will be so close to London, to have a look at the British at the same time and it might even be a wise move to conclude a treaty with King Charles, the British monarch, so that trade between our countries might be facilitated and regulated, leading to an increase of commerce and so, we might hope, to a large increase in Your Majesty's revenue.'

Phra Narai pondered the advice of Phaulkon and found that it was good, for in his heart of hearts, though he hardly admitted this even to himself, Phra Narai believed that Siam would need friends in the future, for if she had no friends was it not just possible that these aggressive Westerners, the British or the French, might come and swallow Siam, battering down the Siamese people with their guns and their trained troops? This was already beginning to happen in India and the princes of India did not seem to be able to resist effectively. Might it not then happen in Siam? The thought was quite unbearable and the King would put it away as soon as it occurred, but it kept recurring and haunted the thinking of Phra Narai.

The King and his Prime Minister were agreed. The French at Paknam were handled with a velvet glove. A mission of imposing proportions was despatched to the court of Versailles and to the court of St. James's—but not everyone viewed with composure the King's attitude towards foreigners. A whisper that was hardly a whisper started to seep through the Palace. At first it was almost negligible. but it grew. It was being said in secrecy that the King had been politically seduced by his Prime Minister, who, after all, was a foreigner himself and who, not unnaturally, had provoked the jealousy of some of the princes and of many of the mandarins.

At this stage the seditious whisper that was percolating through the Palace did not dare to show its face to the sun, and it was not directed, or did not seem to be directed, against the King. Moreover, the secret police, who have always been very efficient in Siam, duly reported the mutterings and the meetings of the dissatisfied mandarins to Phaulkon and the Prime Minister was sufficiently astute and sensitive to the gyroscopic intrigues of his Eastern country to know that such rumours should be treated seriously.

At about this time a man who became famous as Siamese White arrived in Ayuthia. Maurice Collis has written fully and entertainingly of the career of Siamese White and any of my readers who are interested in this extraordinary character are advised to try to get a copy of Collis's enthralling book. White had been summoned to Ayuthia by Phaulkon because there seemed to be a disparity between the amount of merchandise which had been imported into Siam from the ports on the Bay of Bengal, and the amount of revenue which had reached the Exchequer in Ayuthia. White was the Englishman in overall charge of this matter and he was being put on the mat by his superior, Phaulkon, to offer his explanations. Phaulkon by this time had adopted entirely the technique of disapproval common in great Eastern courts. He kept White waiting for ten days before receiving him and then read him a lesson on the responsibilities of his office and the terrible things that might happen to anyone guilty of peculation of the royal funds. White looked round the sumptuous palace of Constantine Phaulkon and no doubt had his own reflections, but from his manner no one could know what they were. He promised instant obedience, assiduous attention to duty and more regular and comprehensive accounting. On these promises Phaulkon allowed him to depart, still securely a Siamese civil servant, and still retaining his important and lucrative post. It should perhaps be explained that high officers of the Crown in Siam at this time, as well as receiving a nominal salary from the government, were permitted by custom to take a percentage of the revenues attaching to their office and to receive gifts. This, of course, was also the practice in China under the Emperor.

Siamese White did not waste the ten days that Phaulkon kept him waiting. He understood immediately why he was not being received. This was an indication of Phaulkon's disapproval and so perhaps an indication that he was not entirely in favour with the King. It was a serious matter, but White was an able and persuasive man and he managed to deal with this little local difficulty most effectively. While he was waiting to be received he moved around Ayuthia talking to high officials and finding out what he could concerning the state of the nation. Phaulkon and White were quite different characters. Phaulkon was a genius at adapting himself to a civilisation that was not his own. He could deal naturally and easily with affairs at the highest level. He was not interested in departmental local affairs. His vision was directed towards Siam as a kingdom and as a going concern. On the personal side only the greatest prizes were regarded as worth grasping and as most of these were in the gift of the King his relationship with Phra Narai was all important to Phaulkon. Perhaps if he had a fault it was that he was too apt to disregard everyone except the King. This was probably a mistake. There were a number of influential princes and ambitious mandarins whom Phaulkon could have cultivated and made his friends. He did not deign to do so. He felt the absolute security that a man feels when he has the implicit trust of an all-powerful head of state and himself controls internal espionage and the means to arrest anyone in the kingdom at any moment.

The astute White sensed that there was something wrong in Ayuthia. He did not think it was directed against the King but he thought it was almost certainly directed against Phaulkon. He had had one or two interviews with the King's council and one or two of the mandarins on this august body gave him the impression that they resented Phaulkon. They did not, of course, say so. It was more by what they did not say, by a gesture here and a look there, that White was able to divine that there might at some time be a move to oust Phaulkon. On the other hand White thought that Phaulkon would probably act first. He had brought his system of secret police and informers up to a very high level. It was, perhaps, the only organisation in Siam that worked with absolute smoothness and efficiency. White had the highest regard for Phaulkon's intelligence. The only question that occurred to White was: Is he getting so big that he will ignore what is going on around him? On the whole White thought that this was most unlikely. The Greek might assume the manners and the modes of a great Siamese nobleman but he retained to the full his native astuteness and caution.

White, on the other hand, decided to learn a lesson, or rather two lessons, from his visit to the capital. First of all he would make his accounting to the treasury much more acceptable. All his papers would be in order. He was a great man for paper work, due perhaps to his early training in the city of London. He did not necessarily mean to cut down his slice of the cake but he proposed to disguise matters very much more effectively. He had been somewhat lax. He had underestimated the grasp which Phaulkon had of the details of every official matter in Siam. During his interview with Phaulkon he had been secretly surprised that Phaulkon had been fully briefed in matters of accounting which White thought were known to him alone. The second lesson which White learned and acted on was that immediate mobility might be very useful to him. By this he meant the ability to leave Siam at a moment's notice with his entire fortune up to date. If anything happened in Ayuthia, if there was a revolution and a new king then, of course, there would be a new prime minister and, according to Siamese custom, everyone connected with the old regime would be 'out', and an entirely new set of officials would be 'in'. It would take some time for the news to reach White but he made sure that if there was any important news from the capital he would be the first to hear about it. And he took one more vitally important step. His large and comfortable bungalow, built of teak, led down to the sea, and White arranged that from the moment of his return onwards three schooners with their crews should be constantly riding at anchor, loaded with his treasure and ready to depart for Britain at a moment's notice.

So we have the situation whereby the two men's positions were entirely different. Phaulkon had a far greater fortune than White could ever hope to have. He was the second most powerful man in Siam, but in order to continue in that position he had to be in Ayuthia, and Ayuthia was fifty-five miles from the sea. White, on the other hand, was living on the Bay of Bengal, a much smaller man by Siamese standards, but a very practical man, with one eye on the collection of the King's revenue in the western provinces and the other eye turned, somewhat apprehensively, towards the capital.

The summer that year was very hot in Ayuthia. There had been hardly any 'mango showers'. The rains could not be expected until July. April was a stifling month. Phra Narai had decided to move out of the capital to witness an elephant hunt when any wild beasts were to be driven in to the keddah and brought into the royal service. It would be cooler in the teak forests of the north. Although the princes of Chiengmai, Chiengrai, Lampang, Lampoon and Nan were semi-independent, the Lord of Life moved in great state with a vast retinue and wherever he went he brought the authority and the power of the central government.

He told Phaulkon of his plans and Phaulkon gave the necessary orders and then, before departing, the King wished to put in order certain affairs during his absence, for instance his uncle would have to act as Regent. This entailed giving an audience to some of the mandarins. The night before this meeting Phaulkon crossed to the palace and sought an urgent interview with the King. Phra Narai, who had just been given a new concubine as a present from the Chow Luang of Chiengmai, did not wish to be disturbed, but Phaulkon insisted.

The King came into the room and said: 'What can it possibly be that cannot wait until the morning?'

Phaulkon handed the King a list of names which the King read in silence. The list included three of the princes and eight of the leading mandarins of the country, including the commander of the palace guard. Phaulkon said: 'These men intend a revolution, Your Majesty. There is no doubt about it. I have checked and checked again. I ask for your permission to arrest them tonight as they are sleeping.'

Phra Narai considered for a moment and then he asked a question: 'Do you think that this is directed against you or is it directed against me as well?'

Phaulkon who, to do him justice, completely identified his own interest with that of the King said: 'I do not know, Your Majesty, but I fear that they intend to change the rulers of Siam.'

Phra Narai: 'I just cannot believe it. They would not dare. I will deal with the matter tomorrow. We have a meeting with the mandarins at noon before our departure and if we see any signs that they intend treason I will allow you to take the steps you desire.'

Phaulkon was greatly agitated by the King's answer. He wanted immediate action. His information indicated that it might be a question of hours only when the initiative would remain in his hands, but the King had turned on his heels and returned to the harem. All Phaulkon could do was to go back to his own palace. He had no authority on his own to carry out the arrests of the men on the list, although he was able to arrest anyone else in Siam. Three of the suspects were princes and were subject only to the King's jurisdiction. The mandarins named were members of the King's council and the practice was for the King to assent before allowing any steps of any nature to be taken against them. Phaulkon almost wished that he had acted on his own initiative and presented the King with a *fait accompli* together with the evidence he had in his possession. Now that the King knew of the matter and had said that he would deal with it the following day there was nothing further that Phaulkon could do.

Phra Narai gave his audience to the mandarins next day. It was his last official act. The mandarins approached the King, moving slowly on all fours, their hands raised above their heads in an attitude of utter humility, loyalty and subjection. Phra Narai, with Phaulkon on his right hand and the commander of the army on his left hand, told the mandarins of his plans for the execution of public affairs while he would be away from the capital and the mandarins appeared to listen to the words of the Lord of Life as they had always done.

But towards the end of the audience, just as Phaulkon was about to dismiss them, one mandarin stood erect. This was an awful and ominous sign and it was a signal. They fell upon Phra Narai and Phaulkon. They took them away and the King was put in a golden sack and beaten to death because they could not touch his body and Phaulkon, not being a royal person, was stabbed to death. It was an assassination of terrible treachery and it had great repercussions, for a new prince was elected King and the party of the mandarins which came to power believed that Siam would best be protected by complete isolation from the world at large. As a result of this the contacts that had been made with Louis XIV of France and with King Charles II of England were abandoned and Siam returned to her own dream world apart and alone.

It was not until the British, who were becoming very active and aggressive in the East, sent Sir John Bowring in 1855 to Siam that a treaty was signed between His Siamese Majesty and Her Britannic Majesty. That treaty ended the period of isolation and it, indirectly, secured the future of Siam as an independent state, for the British were not the only race who were on the path of conquest in the East. The French were also a rising star and they had begun to spread their influence over the princes of Vietnam, of Cambodia and of Laos. The Siamese treaty with the British in effect said to the French 'Hands off Siam', and the French, because they believed that they already had a huge slice of the cake, were prepared to recognise a position in which Siam would be neutral and independent between the British lion and the French tiger.

Would you like to know what happened to the mobile Mr. White? As planned, he was the first to learn of what had happened in Ayuthia. As soon as he heard it he quietly boarded the largest of his vessels and with the other two following in his wake he set sail towards India and the West. As well as his personal fortune in gold and precious stones, he took with him careful copies of his official files and he read these over to himself as he sailed across the Indian Ocean. He was surprised to find that he had slipped up about one small matter. He had murdered an Indian watchman and he had not troubled to have this matter regulated so that the death would appear to be from either natural causes or judicial execution.

However, this matter did not worry him unduly. He was extremely glad that he had got away in time. On the way home, somewhat recklessly, he carried on a war with the ships of the East India Company. White's ships were fully armed and gave a good account of themselves. However, but for an extraordinary piece of good fortune this incident might have led him into real trouble at home, but White was obviously a lucky man. By the time he reached London, four months later, and dropped anchor at Tilbury, the East India Company was out of favour and was being represented in Parliament as being corrupt and dictatorial. This made the freebooters into heroes, at least for the time being, and Siamese White was the classic example of the adventurous English freebooter. He was welcomed in the City and in Whitehall. Here was the type of man whom the English admired. He had initiative, cunning and, now, money. After a delightful stay in London, during which he told the story of his exploits at the court of the King of Siam, he went to the West Country and purchased a manor house, suitably called Plush Court. He settled down to the life of an English country gentleman.

Assassination in Siam, like all other Siamese institutions, has always had a flavour entirely its own.

16

Just Strolling in the Park

IN writing about the Irish one has to be so terribly careful. They have enjoyed being persecuted for centuries
with a masochistic delight. Now that they are not persecuted any longer, and they do not have anybody to blame
for anything except, perish the thought, themselves, life
is not nearly so much fun as it used to be. However, they
manage to enjoy themselves still by carrying round with
them a formidable chip on their protesting shoulders.
And then, of course, they do have some wonderful race-
horses, such as Arkle, who was perhaps more of a hero in
England than he was in Ireland, but then the English are
perverse about these matters, and as they have no in-
feriority complex whatever, they are apt to admire
foreigners and their possessions much more than they do
themselves.

I had recent reason to realise once again that, though
Irish eyes may be smiling and Irish laughter may be a
sheer joy to listen to, neither is prompted by any attempt
at poking fun at the Irish. For instance, in a book entitled *The Great Deceivers*, which is in the same series
as this book, when presenting once again the story of Par-
nell and Kitty O'Shea I wrote these words:

'Your scribe much prefers the tall, cunning, urbane,
ruthless charming men of Ulster to the Blarney-ridden
frauds who seem to inhabit the Irish bogs, including
Dublin.'

Now I would have thought that anyone reading these

words would have suspected that they were not written in deadly earnest, but they seem to have given great offence. I cannot understand this. If something similar had been said about the English they would have said, with a deprecating smile, 'How right you are. That is us exactly.'

The critic of the *Irish Times*, bless it, who signs herself A.K.M. really leapt into the breach when she read my words. Every adjective in the dictionary—titillating, pornographic, repellent—is used to tell her Irish readers what a naughty book *The Great Deceivers* is. Well, I suppose that the review will serve some purpose. It will certainly increase the sales of *The Great Deceivers* both among the tall, cunning, urbane, etc., men of Ulster and the blarney-ridden frauds who inhabit the Irish bogs.

One wonders what the Irish are worried about these days? After all, they have the best of both worlds. They are protected by the British army, navy and air force without paying for it and they have all the advantages, especially the economic advantages, of belonging to the Commonwealth without any of the responsibilities or liabilities which membership from time to time entails. This must suit them down to the ground. Personally I love the Irish. I find their perversity attractive and their maudlin sentimentality when they are drunk very human. When I went over recently to Ireland to take part in the Kilkenny debate I met the most extraordinary characters who seemed to be living in another world, a large and luminous world of their own devising. It was obvious that they regretted losing the English because now they have no one to hate and hatred is essential to an Irishman's happiness. It is no good hating the Germans and the Japanese who have moved in to employ cheap Irish labour, because these races are really not worth hating, but the British one can hate with satisfaction and the fact that they do not mind being hated makes it all the more intolerable.

I think one of the things that the Irish miss, though they would deny it with a roar of protest, is the grandeur and the glamour which the British brought into their lives, which was, of course, exemplified by and reached its apex in Viceregal Lodge in the old days of the British Raj.

To understand the evil and unnecessary assassination which forms the subject of this chapter one has to know, or remind oneself, of the outline of Irish history.

Most of this has been so twisted and distorted in the history books, especially by Irish writers, that it is sometimes difficult to remind oneself what the real facts were.

For instance, Oliver Cromwell is often presented as the scourge of the Irish. In fact Cromwell, by the standards of the day, treated the Irish extremely well.

On the death of Charles I, Charles II was proclaimed King in Ireland in several places, and his cousin Prince Rupert landed at Kinsale. On the 28th of March 1649 Oliver Cromwell was named Lord Lieutenant of Ireland and landed in August with an army of eight thousand foot and four thousand horse, besides artillery, and a military chest of twenty thousand pounds, a large sum in those days. Jones, who held Dublin, was second-in-command and Ireton was third-in-command. Cromwell at once issued orders directing all acts of private vengeance to be forbidden, and ordering that all provisions, etc., should be fully paid for. His proclamation stated: 'We are come to ask an account for the innocent blood that has been shed, and to endeavour to bring to an account all who by appearing in arms shall justify the same.' Cromwell kept to his own orders, but, of course, when he was resisted, as he was by Ormond at Drogheda, Cromwell attacked furiously and no quarter was given on either side. Even so, he regretted when his troops departed from his own written order. He said: 'I believe the Friars were knocked on the head promiscuously, and this should not be.'

In the main Cromwell's statement stands without dispute: 'Since my coming into Ireland not a man not in arms has been massacred, destroyed or burned.' In nine months, in one of the most brilliant campaigns of history,

he restored order and peace to Ireland. After marching
from victory to victory Cromwell could leave the island
on the 29th of May 1650 for work that awaited him in
England, leaving his son-in-law Ireton behind him as Lord
Deputy.

One of the outstanding matters which Cromwell left
behind was the bringing to justice of the prisoners who
had been guilty of the massacre of 1641. This was later
accomplished and about two hundred, after a scupul-
ously fair trial, were executed. Henry Cromwell, the son
of the Protector, finalised the settlement of Ireland. It was
decided to introduce apartheid into Ireland. The Irish
Catholic gentry, or rather all those who had borne arms
against the Parliament, were transported with their servants and cattle beyond the Shannon, which was to serve
as the boundary of the new pale. These and other measures
invoked the hatred of the Irish, and Irish children, when
they were disobedient, were threatened with the curse of
Cromwell. Autonomy was abolished, thirty Irish Members being sent to the joint Parliament of the Three King-
doms of Westminster. Cromwell's rule and Cromwell's
measures gave Ireland five years of good government and
practically the only peaceful period she was to enjoy until
the present day. The Irish Members of Parliament were to
enliven the debates at Westminster and play havoc with
the rules of procedure and the British Establishment for
many years. The mentality of the Irish M.P.s was entirely
different from the average English Member of Parliament,
who tended to be somewhat pompous and conservative
whatever party he belonged to.

The Irish members were not like this at all. They were
more like scurrilous schoolboys and they never tired of
thinking of ways and means of promoting mischief and
annoying the authorities. The cause which the Irish
Members sponsored was that of Irish independence, but
the Irish, by their own behaviour, did not seem fit for self-
government. The time had not come when it was possible
for the world to realise that people preferred to govern

themselves badly rather than to be well governed by a superior alien civilisation. Of course, there were writers who supported the Irish cause. Swift was one of these and later Chesterfield wrote: 'The poor of Ireland are worse used than Negroes by their masters.' The cause of independence was probably helped by the terrible tragedy that from time to time ravaged the Irish people. For instance, in 1739 a famine resulted from a very bad potato crop and it is said that almost a fifth of the population of Ireland perished, but even such a disaster did not dispose the Irish to work with the English. When England began to make proposals for renewing the Union as under Cromwell the whole country protested and an armed mob of many thousands broke into the Houses of Parliament on College Green, and were not dispersed without military force and much bloodshed. The situation was largely the fault of the Irish Parliament itself, which was hopelessly corrupt. Almost anything could be achieved by sinecures and pensions. It was not until the coming of Burke into the English Parliament and Grattan into the Irish that the tone and tenor of Irish political life altered for the better.

The story of Irish Independence is long and complicated, but it did seem that Pitt had finalised the question. He was disgusted with the bloodstained past. He decided to buy the Irish politicians and he did so with over a million pounds of gold, so that in June 1800 Ireland became at last an integral part of the United Kingdom, contributing one hundred members to the joint House of Commons and twenty-eight representative peers with four Bishops. The formal proclamation of the Union took place on the 1st of January 1801 and the Union Jack received the saltire cross of St. Patrick blended with the saltire cross of St. Andrew in addition to the well-known upright cross of St. George.

This should have been the end of the matter, but nothing ever satisfied the Irish and in July 1803 a man called Robert Emmet contrived a revolt in Dublin with the object of seizing the Castle. Emmet's revolt did not meet with success and eventually he was caught and executed for treason.

Daniel O'Connell, the Irish leader, formed a very widespread Catholic Association in Ireland, and the Duke of Wellington, at this time Prime Minister, seeing quite clearly that the Catholic legal inabilities would lead to civil war, practically commanded the hesitating House of Lords to pass the Roman Catholic Emancipation Act, which they did on the 13th of April 1829. This entailed altering the oath of public office and thereafter Catholics were free to hold all offices except those of Regent, Lord Chancellor and Lord Lieutenant.

The year 1845 saw another terrible famine in Ireland and the political climate started to deteriorate once more, the real complaint being that the very large and indigenous Catholic majority was being made subject to quite a small Protestant minority. In 1850 the Fienian brotherhood was founded in America and it was this organisation that, directly or indirectly, fought the long and bloody guerilla campaign that eventually resulted in Ireland securing a unique position as a foreign part of the United Kingdom. This great backlog of historical hatred is the only excuse one can give for the murderous treachery which from time to time disfigured the public life of Ireland. It almost seemed, to the English at any rate, that the Irish preferred to shoot people in the back rather than to confront them face to face. And many of the murders seemed to be timed with the sole view of aggravating animosity. For instance, in 1873 Mr. Isaac Butt started the Home Rule party, so that from this moment onwards the cause of Home Rule could be pressed and sponsored in a perfectly legitimate and parliamentary manner which was bound in the end to prove effective. Moreover, an Irish National Association for the reduction of rents called the Land League was formed, though this League promoted outrages and disturbances and had to be suppressed in 1881. The grievances which underlay these indications of discontent had just been investigated and numerous reforms were effected. The land laws were remodelled in 1870 and then more thoroughly and completely in 1881. So that to the impartial observer not involved in the torrid malice and hatred of Irish politics, it really looked as if, at long last, Ireland was coming into her own and that there was hope for her in the future.

Then occurred an event similar in essence to what had occurred again and again in Irish history whenever peace seemed in sight, giving the texture of the Irish tragedy the inevitability of a Greek drama. Early in May 1882 Lord Frederick Cavendish, who, of course, belonged to the family of the Duke of Devonshire, sailed for Ireland as Chief Secretary to the Lord Lieutenant, in succession to Mr. Forster. Lord Frederick, who was a man of much culture and amiability, went for a stroll in Phoenix Park with the Permanent Under-Secretary, a Mr. Burke. Both men, of course, were unsuspecting and unarmed. They had no guard of any kind. The recent moves towards religious emancipation, famine relief and land reform and the very large Irish representation at Westminster had lulled Vice-regal Lodge into believing that at last the great divide was over and the anger and the hatred were a thing of the past.

Five men sprang out from some bushes and murdered Lord Frederick Cavendish and Mr. Burke by shooting them down like dogs. Both men were not yet dead but both were obviously dying. The five Irish heroes vanished over the wall to be secreted and succoured by their friends. They were not caught. A new and terrible chapter in the history of Anglo-Irish relations had begun.

It is not true to say that assassination never accomplishes anything. In certain circumstances, where passions have died or at least are only smouldering, a well-timed and brutal assassination can restore hatred and evil more effectively than any other single act could hope to do. Such was the case when the two Englishmen fell dying in Phoenix Park. It is an assassination still vividly remembered and because of its cowardly brutality must always be regarded as a shameful and horrible plot.

17

Death of a Saint

MOHANDAS KARAMCHAND GANDHI came from a family that belonged to the Banya, the trading caste, of India, who were followers of the Vaishnava sect. This sect was influenced by Jainism, which meant that its followers hated the taking of life. From this it followed that they never ate meat or fowl or fish.

The family were quite prosperous, as was fairly common for the middle class of Indian merchants. The British confined themselves to ruling the country through the Civil Service and the army and the law courts with the police. British trade was carried on at the highest level, usually by very large firms. Virtually the whole of the retail trade in all the bazaars, catering to the needs of three hundred million Indians, was in Indian hands and this allowed considerable wealth to accumulate to industrious commercial families such as the one from which Gandhi came.

There was, however, a good deal of snobbery not only among the British in India but also among the Indians. It was usually quite harmless. On the British side it divided society into the armed services, with the provincial governors, the military commanders and the Viceroy at the apex, and the commercial community, who were referred to somewhat disparagingly—and quite unjustly—as 'box-wallahs'. On the Indian side the professions were always regarded as being superior to trade. And of all the pro-

fessions it was the law that chiefly attracted the ambitious
and affluent young Indian. A very limited number of able
young Indians were able to enter the Civil Service, and,
of course, for the military castes, there was the army. The
young Indian gentlemen who became officers in the
Indian regiments adopted a very special philosophy and
attitude towards life, and indeed they still do.

This being the background it was not surprising that
young Gandhi should be sent to London, where, at the
rather early age of nineteen, he was called to the Bar.
His success in sitting for both parts of the Bar exam
showed that he had two capabilities—he spoke English
fluently and read it equally well, and he had a good memory and a nimble wit. 'Eating dinners' was something of a
trial to him, for he could neither enjoy the roast beef nor
indulge in the wine, but no doubt his manners were im-
peccable, and, as the students dined in messes of four,
non-drinking Asian students were quite popular with their
English opposite numbers, who were quite prepared to
drink their share of the Temple wine for them. The
records we have suggest that Gandhi rather enjoyed his
stay in Britain, most of which he spent in London.

On returning to his own country he immediately started to practise law, but at the age of twenty-four some
Indian clients, who had a large trade with South Africa,
asked him to go to that country to settle a dispute they had
concerning a rice shipment. He must have been an extraordinary young man because after he had been in the
country a few weeks the leaders of the Indian community
asked him to stay and join the fight for the rights of
Indians trading and working in South Africa. At this time
there was a very rigid colour bar and Asian residents suffered all kinds of restrictions and indignities. Gandhi does
not seem to have been over-impressed with non-violence
at this point in his career, although he undoubtedly felt
strongly about the futility of war. He initiated an Indian
stretcher-bearer corps which served with distinction
throughout the Boer War. To some extent at any rate

he was identifying himself with the British. It was much later when great events induced him to devote his life to peaceful but powerful resistance of British rule.

The character of the man who became world famous as Mahatma Gandhi is the subject of fierce if muted controversy. His opponents said that he had in an excessive degree the litigious and devious mentality of the Hindu lawyer. They doubted his motives and believed that at all times he was scheming to get power into his own hands. They said that his abhorrence of violence was merely part of the negative tradition of Hinduism and Jainism and that he could never be trusted to keep his word. Moreover, they were quite sure that he was not basically an especially good or moral person and in support of this criticism they stated that as he grew older, he was accustomed to sleep between two girls in a tradition derived from the princes of India. They admit that money did not interest him, so that on this score he could not be attacked. He was incorruptible in the financial sense because it was power not money that he sought. His critics went on to say that, as long as British rule in India was firm and apparently there to stay, Gandhi supported the British Raj, but as soon as it weakened and was obviously going to go, he deserted his benefactors and placed himself at the head of the popular revolutionary movement; at the same time he sought to escape any responsibility for the chaos and violence and murder that might ensue by declaring his movement to be entirely pacific. This is not a flattering picture of a man, but is it true?

Undoubtedly Gandhi had a subtle Hindu mind, as one would expect an able young Hindu lawyer to possess. There was nothing unnatural or odd about this. He did not think as an Englishman thinks or act as an Englishman acts, and it would have been suspicious had he done so. In matters of sex Indians have quite different standards from most Europeans and even if it was true that Gandhi, the ascetic, had young girls with him this means very little. There is throughout the East a belief that ageing men can restore their vitality by a contiguous relationship with young women. To the Eastern mind there is nothing improbable about this, but, of course, Western critics will often meet any such suggestion with cynical incredulity. In the same way there seems little point in attempting to denigrate Gandhi because he did not accept the money values. Equally he did not accept the religion of force. Nor did he accept the British class-system or its equivalent the Indian caste-system. He was deliberately and provocatively out of step with the kind of values that held sway in India under the British Raj and the princes of India.

I find this rebellion at all levels against what he considered false standards admirable. I do not think he was a hypocrite in either political, social or sexual matters. The fact that, with few exceptions, the British did not understand him does not make him inexplicable. In order to understand Gandhi we have to understand the Hindu mind.

Hinduism is a delightfully vague religion or way of life and does not attempt to determine the purpose of God. The Hindus take some pride in the fact that their faith is not attached to historical personalities. They pay little regard to the dynastic trend of world history with its battles, its revolutions, and its great men. They find this whole panorama of history often proves to be an illusion. So that having a faith founded largely on a negative they are apt to regard as their hero the ascetic who has renounced the world. It was into this slot that Gandhi was eventually to fit so comfortably.

India had always been a hot-bed of religious fervour. From time to time over the centuries some great leader had attempted to merge the religions of the country into one overall Indian faith. But they had always failed. For instance, Akbar the Great, who ruled in Delhi as Emperor between 1556 and 1605, attempted to form a universal religion by combining Hinduism, Buddhism, Islam, Zoroastrianism and Christianity. This was a magnificent conception but clearly at least five hundred years ahead of its time. Kabir, one of the greatest of the fifteenth-century teachers, was a strong critic of Hindu polytheism and to this extent, without abandoning his own religion, he tended to stretch out a hand towards Islam. And throughout the history that followed great men in India attempted to close the gap on the one hand between Hinduism and Mohamedanism and on the other, between the high caste Hindus and the other castes, including even the casteless untouchables. The great Indian poet Tagore attacked negative asceticism complaining that those who devoted themselves exclusively to world-renunciation were as selfish as those who devoted themselves solely to the pursuit of wealth.

In the case of Mahatma Gandhi he singled out the Indian ethical virtue of 'Ahimsa', which he interpreted as universal compassion, though one must admit that when it came to politics Gandhi subscribed fully to the dictum that politics is the science of what can actually be achieved.

During the twenty years he was in South Africa Gandhi fought and won his battle against the authorities. He was imprisoned on three occasions, but he was a most unsatisfactory prisoner because he had the gift of withdrawing completely from the world of his surroundings and this was apt to disconcert his warders. He achieved practically everything he set out to achieve. He obtained the repeal of the three-pound annual tax upon ex-indentured coolies in Natal. The whole status of the Indian community in South Africa was raised and placed on a firm foundation and Indian marriages were made valid under South African law.

On his return to his own country he established an ashram at Ahmadabad in Gujarat. This was a retreat from the world. It consisted of the simplest wooden buildings which were roofed by dried ferns cut from the local jungle, which incidentally were a good protection against excessive heat and the rains of the monsoon. Gandhi and his followers did without almost everything. Their diet was vegetarian and extremely simple, requiring very little cooking. Their clothes consisted of a dhoti which they spun themselves. They employed no machinery whatever. Their exercise was walking. Their habit was meditation and they practised a modified form of yoga.

An old friend of mine who remembers the Gandhi of this period says that it was an extraordinary sight to see the Mahatma in the evening surrounded by his followers, which usually included one or two English ladies attracted presumably by the aura of sanctity. Gandhi would talk when the spirit moved him and his voice was clear and effortless, like the song of a bird. His ascendency over his followers was absolute. He was able to establish a complete serenity. No violence, no frustration, no annoyance, no temper and no passion intruded on the idyllic scene. My friend thought it was a little dull but then there are people who think that heaven, if we ever get there, is going to have its dull moments. In any case, Gandhi was going to be torn from his retreat by turbulent and public events. He was still very much a supporter of British rule. In the first world war, following the pattern he had adopted in South Africa, he enlisted a labour corps for service and for this effort he received the Kaisar-i-Hind medal.

The event that changed his whole life was the killing and wounding of a large number of people by British troops under the command of General Dyer at the Jalianwalla Bagh in Amritsa on the 13th of April 1919. I am one of those who believe that General Dyer acted as he should have acted in firing on the large and dangerous and partially armed mob who had already burnt two police stations. Had he not done so it might well have been that murder and arson would have been loosed on the city of Amritsa and thousands of unfortunate people could have met their death. The crowd had been warned three times to disperse and had refused. General Dyer left it to the very last moment before acting. The British government, instead of supporting him, turned against him for this singular service and made him the scapegoat of their own ambiguous Indian policies. However, to Gandhi the 'massacre' of Amritsa was a turning point in his life. He was profoundly stirred and joined those who urged the boycott of the council set up under the Montagu-Chelmsford reforms. He toured the country urging Indians to give up all titles and offices and to refuse to work as government officials or to attend school or to pay taxes. The boycott was extended to foreign cloth and everyone was urged to wear the *khaddar*, which became world famous as the Gandhi cap. Gandhi's idea was that this non-violent, non-co-operation, which went under the name of *satyagraha*, or soul-force, would paralyse the British government and force them to grant immediate Home Rule.

From now on Gandhi's life was no longer that of the religious ascetic but rather that of the astute demagogue who exercised immense power over the masses of India. It seemed that whenever the relationship between the British and the Indians was going to improve some event was bound to shatter the reconciliation. For instance, in 1921 riots broke out in Bombay at the time of the welcome to the Prince of Wales and over fifty people were killed. This was a ghastly tragedy, for the Prince of Wales had been an immensely successful ambassador for Britain round the world and his charm was such that the people of India would certainly have responded to him had the visit not been marred by this terrible event.

In fact Gandhi had released forces that he could not control. A year later in the United Provinces a mob set fire to the police barracks and burned the occupants alive. In 1924 Gandhi and his immediate political associates, including Nehru, were arrested. Nehru has left us a most striking account of these arrests. On the morning in question something in the atmosphere told Gandhi and his followers that the British were going to act against them and in fact when the police cars drove up to the house where they all were Gandhi and all the others had already packed, so certain were they that the premonition was right. Gandhi was sentenced to six years' imprisonment and was detained for a time in one of the Aga Khan's palaces. Before this he was sent to an ordinary prison. He was always fasting or threatening to fast 'unto death', but he never pursued the matter, because the British, who appeared to have had some kind of affection for him, or perhaps respect, invariably released him when things began to look dangerous.

When the second world war broke out Gandhi started by giving Britain limited support in the teeth of strong Congress opposition, for he had a great hatred of Nazism, which, of course, embodied and enshrined violence as a god, but as the war went on Gandhi's view changed and he persisted in attempting to obstruct the war effort. He was imprisoned again, but from his prison he carried on a correspondence with the Viceroy, protesting against the arrest of himself and his followers. Again he undertook a last fast but again he was unconditionally released on the ground of ill-health in May 1944.

So came the second turning point in his life. Gandhi now retired from active politics. Nehru largely took over as the active political leader. But Gandhi was to embark upon a last and, as it turned out, fatal campaign.

All the efforts that had been made throughout the centuries to still the enmity between Hindu and Moslem had failed and in 1945, on the verge of independence, it appeared that the hatred of the centuries which British rule had been able to control and to subject was going to break out into a blood-bath of unbelievable proportions. The remedy for this as conceived by Lord Mountbatten, the last British Viceroy, was to partition India into two independent and sovereign states, India and Pakistan, the first being predominantly Hindu and the latter being mainly Moslem. Thus the unifying work of a hundred and fifty years of British rule, making the Indians into one great nation, would be undone overnight, but perhaps this was worth while in order to avoid mass genocide. In the event this was not avoided because at one time it was estimated there were nearly four million refugees on the move and they were slaughtered in incredible numbers and with unbelievable ferocity.

The whole of Gandhi's life at this moment seemed to lie in ruins, for he foresaw what would happen if partition was attempted. He knew that the real basis and alleged justification for partition was a deep and bitter religious strife between Hindu and Moslem, and he set out to tour Bengal on foot, his message being one calculated to stir up bitter resentment among the fanatics of both sides, for his message was one of peace and a plea for Hindu-Moslem unity.

Bengal has always had a reputation for whispered intrigues and sudden awful violence. The climate seems to be conducive to this kind of horror. In spite of this, and in spite of constant mutterings and murmurings from both sides, Gandhi carried on his campaign. He walked all the morning from one village to another arriving before the sun had reached its zenith. Then he would rest and in the evening address the multitude. There was something very biblical in the manner of his progress and although clearly he did not carry conviction with everyone, he was making great headway and the watching eyes and ears of the most fanatical of the Hindus feared that once again this extraordinary little man by the force of his personality and by the inspiration of his words might swing India behind him. Had he done so one of the greatest tragedies of the twentieth century might have been avoided. But he could not be allowed to succeed. In a back room in a slum in Delhi the leaders of that rigid inner core of the Hindu faith met and decided that Gandhi must die. This was an awful decision and reflected the burning hatred of the party of Hindu orthodoxy for any change or compromise whatever.

They chose a youth to do the murder for them and on the 30th of January 1948, as Gandhi was walking slowly through a crowd who sought to touch his garment, on his way to a prayer meeting at New Delhi, the assassin struck and the man who had won the heart of India sank to his feet dying.

It is a tribute perhaps to the century of discipline and strictly enforced 'justice' imposed by the British that the young assassin was not lynched on the spot as he would have been in nearly all Eastern countries and perhaps in some Western countries. The huge concourse of people, that grew every moment as the news of this awful tragedy spread far and wide, allowed the police to arrest the killer and to take him away. At first the crowd seemed stunned and then, realising what had happened, a great wail went up, a noise such as is only heard in Eastern countries expressing lamentation and sorrow in its direst form.

The young man whom the police carried away was a nondescript, slim, quietly dressed Indian, quite unnoticeable in a crowd. In order to attract even less attention he had taken the precaution of wearing a Gandhi cap. It never occurred to anyone that he was not a friend. His life story was sordid and pitiful. As an apprentice he had been beaten regularly by his master, so that every week or so he would be seen outside the little tanning factory weeping bitterly and nursing his bruises. He fled from this persecution and joined the men who afterwards used him to kill Gandhi. They flattered him, telling him that his name would go down in history. It never did go down in history. Neither his original name nor the name he later assumed are ever mentioned in India. His memory was perpetuated only by the shroud of silent ignominy.

I remember vividly hearing the news in Bangkok and sharing to some extent the feeling of outrage and horror that all Indians felt. I had seen Gandhi going to a conference in Whitehall, walking from his London hotel in 1930, a hopping, sprightly little figure in his crumpled dhoti with his great hooked nose and luminous eyes, like a white bird skimming along the pavement, his staff, which he always carried, assisting him. Perhaps nowadays when odd clothes are not unusual he would not have made so bizarre an impression, but in the London of the thirties he was the strangest figure imaginable. It was as if Christ or one of his disciples had suddenly decided to visit London on a reincarnation.

There has never been a funeral quite like the funeral of Mahatma Gandhi. There seemed to be very little body to burn on the immense funeral pyre, and very few ashes to scatter on the holy Ganges, but for a day not only India but the whole world held its breath, for they realised that this was the passing of a man whose like they might never see again.

Gandhi had gone and India wept. His assassin was tried, convicted and sentenced, but they never did discover who the men were behind this ferocious and evil deed, so that we may assume that the same forces and the same fanaticism are lurking there today as sinister as they were when they struck Mahatma Gandhi on that beautiful cool January evening in 1948.

18

An Old English Custom

WE are apt to think, these days, that assassination is for foreigners only, essentially an alien custom, quite out of place in the British democracy where we get rid of our prime ministers by voting against the party which they lead in the House of Commons. Yet there was a time when assassination seemed part of the fabric of British life and the extraordinary story of Thomas A'Becket, his friendship with King Henry II and their long and involved political estrangement brings back to us very vividly twelfth-century England when the assassination of an archbishop by a king in England did not seem outrageous but fitted into the violent epoch and to the passionate political and religious power struggles of the time. In order to understand the dreadful deed that was committed in Canterbury Cathedral on the 29th of December 1170—the spot is still marked on the Cathedral floor—we must know something about A'Becket and his long relationship with the King.

Thomas A'Becket was born of English parents in 1117 in London where his father, Gilbert, was a merchant. He was first educated at Merton Abbey, in Surrey, and afterwards at London, Oxford and Paris. When employed in the office of the Sheriff of London his manners and talents recommended him to Theobald, Archbishop of Canterbury, an acquaintance of his father, by whom he was sent to study civil law, first under Gratian at Bologna, and then at Auxerre in Burgundy. On his return his patron gave

him the livings of St. Mary-le-Strand, London, and Otte-
ford in Kent, and sent him to manage the business of the
see of Canterbury at the court of Rome.

His success recommended him powerfully both to the
archbishop and to King Henry II, who made him his intimate and familiar associate, and created him chancellor
in 1158—A'Becket being the first Englishman after the
Conquest who was appointed to any high office—and
subsequently, in 1162, after some opposition, Archbishop
of Canterbury. Henry wished to subject the clergy to the
authority of the civil courts for murder, felony, and similar
crimes, and no doubt thought that A'Becket would be his
ready helper in so just and patriotic an effort, for, as a
contemporary chronicler says, 'the world had never seen
two friends so thoroughly of one mind as the king and
him' (Roger de Pontigny).

But A'Becket, favourite as he was—loaded with every
possible honour and possession by his friend—warned
him that as primate he 'would have to choose between the
favour of God and that of the king', and the greatest opposition to his appointment came from himself. The struggle
was as clear to A'Becket as it soon became to Henry. The
powerful Pope Gregory VII (elected 1073), a monk who
realised the visions of the cloister, had shaken off the yoke
so long borne, and freed the Papacy from its subserviency
to imperial authority. But Gregory had even gone further,
and claimed authority over the secular princes. Henry,
awake to the life-and-death struggle for supremacy, endeavoured in 1164 to get the consent of the Archbishop
to the celebrated 'Constitutions of Clarendon', which
were drawn up to bring back the clergy under the jurisdiction of the realm, as it existed in the time of 'my grand-
father, Henry I'.

This at first A'Becket refused to give, with passionate
denial, but he was at length forced to comply. When asked
to sign as well as swear, he revoked his oath, and obtained
absolution for this from the Pope; then, finding himself
the object of the King's displeasure, he attempted to

escape to France, upon which Henry summoned a Parliament at Northampton in 1165, and charged him with breaking his allegiance. He was fined heavily, and a demand for his accounts as chancellor was made; for he had resigned the chancellorship almost at once after becoming archbishop, in order the more completely to devote his services to the work of the Church—at the same time abruptly changing his habits of life from those of a luxurious courtier to those of a monkish ascetic.

After openly defying the King and the council in a violent scene, he escaped to France where he continued to maintain with great vigour his own rights and those which he alone, not supported even by the Pope, asserted to belong to the Church. At length a reconciliation was effected in 1170, at Freteville on the borders of Touraine, and the King restored A'Becket to his see with all its privileges. But he was rash enough immediately to publish the suspension of the Archbishop of York and the excommunication of all the bishops who had taken part in the coronation of Henry's eldest son. (This prince was also called Henry, and afterwards died before his father and co-sovereign.) A'Becket had traded on the King's ill-health and the necessity the King was under of crowning young Henry, to make clear the succession—an act which he as primate alone could perform. Regardless of the Pope's express orders to his fellow archbiships to do what he himself refused to do (unless under conditions impossible for the King to yield), A'Becket sent secret messengers before himself bearing his decrees, and England was at once aflame.

The King, who was then in Normandy, is said to have expressed his vexation that none of his followers had revenged him on this insolent priest. Reginald Fitzurse, William de Tracy, Hugh de Moreville, and Richard Brito, four barons, accordingly formed a resolution either to effect the submission or the death of the Archbishop. On the 29th of December 1170 they attacked him in the Cathedral of Canterbury, out of which they tried to drag him, but he clung to a pillar near the high altar, grappled with de Tracy and almost threw him down. Fitzurse aimed a blow at him which slightly wounded him, but broke the arm of Edward Grim, his cross-bearer. The Archbishop then putting himself in a devout posture, the blows of the other assassins clove his skull and scattered his brains over the pavement.

As we recall the strange and violent story of Thomas A'Becket and the King the gigantic stature of Thomas A'Becket and the strength of his character seem to reach down to us through the long catalogue of English history.

Let us end our enquiry into the great assassins by recalling one other case at the very dawn of the Norman Conquest, the death of William Rufus in the New Forest on the 2nd of August 1100. A great deal has been written about this since the exhaustive work on William's reign by Professor Freeman, but it is still being suggested that a French knight named Walter Tyrell shot at a stag and that the arrow hit a tree from which it glanced and mortally wounded William. It is an ingenious theory and might account for the fact that William was shot in the back, but personally I do not believe a word of it.

All we know about the Red King, who loved the red deer as if he was their father, suggests that he was the kind of man who would collect enemies like other men collect the trophies of war.

Even his friends said that he was vicious, blasphemous, rapacious, violent, lustful, but they added that he always kept his knightly word and was kind to his friends. I am not quite sure what this means, but if this was all that they could find to say in praise of their monarch he must have been a rather dreadful kind of person.

Certainly from the beginning he was overbearing, cunning and wilful. He was born in Normandy in 1057, the second son of his father, but he overrode Robert, the eldest son, and got himself crowned by Archbishop Lanfranc at Westminster on the 26th day of September 1087.

He was just thirty years of age. So odious was he to all and sundry that his uncles, Odo, Bishop of Bayeux, and the Earl of Montaigne, rebelled against him almost at once, assisted by Robert, but the Red King crushed them with his relentless determination.

Rufus was forty-three when he died and, looking at the incident even from this distance, there can, I think, be little doubt that he was assassinated by an enemy. If indeed it was an accident one would have expected his friends to have stayed with his body, but later in the day some colliers passing through the New Forest near Minstead found his dead body lying on the ground, transfixed by an arrow which had passed through to his breast. They conveyed the body next day to Winchester in their cart and it was buried in the cathedral there.

There were few tears shed in England for the death of the Red King.

Assassination is, of course, the outward and visible sign of a lack of stable democratic government and the acceptance of standards of violence as part of political life. As we have seen, the assassinations of Lincoln and Kennedy show this very clearly. The age of the gun is passing in America, but it has not yet passed. Every now and again there are men in the United States who get tired of 'shuffling papers' and believe that the bullet is the real answer.

I think that, in attempting to sum up, we must say that assassination is never the answer. Violence breeds violence and in this book we have a strange and horrible instance of this in the case of General Qasim, who met retribution for the assassination of his King in so dreadful a manner. It would be dangerous to say that assassination is on the way out, for this assumes that democracy is on the way in. Is it? At least this is open to doubt. In the African continent alone some eight military dictatorships have been launched in the last ten years, and the elimination of some of these dictators by assassination seems likely to be the story of tomorrow.

Finally, it may be worth remembering that assassination is murder whether the motive is a political one or not. Perhaps the word assassination suggests that the murderers can conceivably be excused because their motives are different from those of the domestic murderer but, in my opinion, they can never be excused or pardoned, for the taking of life is the ultimate sin against the light.

19

Where There is no Vision
the People Perish

HEATHROW Airport, London, is the busiest inter-national airport in the world. Saturday, June 8th, 1968, was one of the busiest days of the year. It was almost the height of the holiday season and the huge traffic in passengers of all nationalities was reaching a crescendo. It was, therefore, an extremely alert Customs official who asked a passenger from Lisbon, who had just arrived by BEA Trident jet en route to Brussels, to step into the office for some routine enquiries. Enquiries there were, but they were not routine, for the man who gave his name as Ramon George Sneyd seemed to the Customs man to bear a marked resemblance to the photograph of James Earl Ray whom the FBI had been looking for since the murder of Martin Luther King on a fine spring day in Memphis, an assassination that had shocked the world. Sneyd was travelling with a Canadian passport and this was the key to his arrest.

Scotland Yard's 'C' Department moved in, fingerprinted the suspect and quickly established that Sneyd was in fact James Earl Ray, a forty-year-old escaped convict who also went under the extraordinary name of Eric Starvo Galt, accused of assassinating Dr. King on April 4th in Memphis.

For an escaped convict, presumably not flush with funds, Ray had proved extremely mobile. His escape from Memphis up to the moment of his detention in London would appear to be incredible unless he was backed by money and some kind of organisation, not necessarily political, possibly criminal.

Ray had left his fingerprints on the Remington rifle that is reported to have killed Dr. King. Again this appears to be strangely careless unless, of course, he was quite certain that he could get away from the scene of the shooting.

In so far as it has been possible to trace his movements since April 4th, it appears that Sneyd flew to Toronto on April 8th where he obtained a Canadian passport. On the 6th of May he flew to London by BOAC and on the 7th he flew on to Portugal. Meanwhile a gigantic manhunt had been launched by the FBI who had sent emissaries to Canada and Mexico, regarded as the most likely places for Ray to seek to hide. No expense was spared in this major police effort and it is fair to say that the FBI received magnificent co-operation. For example the Royal Canadian Mounted Police checked over a quarter of a million passport photographs comparing them with a photograph of the man alleged to be the killer. They had checked over ninety thousand photographs without a clue. Then one came up and, although the type of face was not unusual, the cleft chin in conjunction with an oddly shaped nose made the investigator pause. This was it.

Why Ray chose to fly back to London even if it was his intention to proceed to Brussels probably nobody knows but the man himself. At the Canadian Embassy in Lisbon he managed to obtain a new passport on the grounds that his name had been misspelled on the existing one. Under Canadian law, passports are given very freely and on the minimum of evidence. Only the Canadian nationality of the applicant has to be established and the official is empowered to accept the applicant's word for this. So that when Ray flew into London he had two passports. He also had a considerable sum of money and an automatic pistol—which was loaded.

Ray was placed in custody at Cannon Row police station

and security measures were taken to make quite sure that this man, whom the police regarded as dangerous, and now desperate, would not escape. Back home Ray faced a murder indictment and a federal conspiracy charge. His apprehension and detention were a major achievement for international law enforcement co-operation.

Had Ray not been arrested one more terrible question mark might have hung indefinitely over the murder of Martin Luther King. Dr. King was the acknowledged leader of moderate Negro opinion in the United States. This made him the spokesman for some thirty million American citizens. He was a man of vision and he was, to the end, a believer in non-violence in his campaign to bring black America on to a level with white America. Eight years ago he had been awarded the Nobel Peace Prize for his lifetime of service to his people and for his services to peace. He was by far the most distinguished American Negro in the political field. This being so it was inevitable, given the political climate of the last decade, that Martin Luther King's life should be in constant danger. He received a dozen serious death threats a week and obscene telephone calls beyond counting, but he carried on, certain of his mission, sure of his vision which was a greater America in which white and black would work together in harmony and mutual respect.

There was nothing to suggest that he was more in danger on April 4th, 1968, than he had been for many years. In fact, he was coming to be regarded as an American institution and the American people do not like their institutions to be blotted out.

The issue that brought Dr. King to Memphis was not one of national importance. It was a local issue. Sanitation workers were staging a strike for fairly modest wage increases. The majority of these men were Negroes. The mayor, a Mr. Henry Loeb, had turned down the workers' demands and this had been followed by some Negro looting. The response to this was to call in State Troopers and National Guardsmen. This was the kind of climate that

Martin Luther King hated. He believed that once violence had been resorted to, reason flew out of the window. However, he stayed on in Memphis in case he might be able to help when the atmosphere became less tense. He stayed at a motel on Mulberry Street called the Lorraine which had two storeys and was owned by a Negro. It was also close to Mason Street where the demonstration of the sanitation workers had started.

Across the street from the Lorraine is a rooming house which is divided into two parts, one for its white patrons, one for its black. Mrs. Bessie Brewer remembers booking in a man who called himself John Willard who paid his eight-dollar rent in advance with a twenty-dollar bill. Willard chose a room overlooking Mulberry Street and immediately opposite the first floor balcony of the Lorraine.

Dr. King had been having a session with his advisers. They had been discussing plans for the new march. As soon as the session was over he went to wash and change for dinner. He decided to relax and chat with his friends on the outside balcony. It was getting cool as the sun went down and King's driver, Solomon Jones, persuaded Dr. King to put on his overcoat. He was buttoning it up as the shots rang out. King's friends knew what that meant. It meant death in the evening. Following what had now become routine for them they fell flat on the ground in case a fusillade should follow. They looked at their leader. A bullet had entered his right jaw and cut through his spinal cord. The impact was so great that he was flattened upright against the back wall of the balcony. He raised his hands to his head, then he crashed forward on the ground, dying. Blood spurted from his mouth and nose and even from his ears. The wound itself was also gushing blood. King's friends did their best to stop the bleeding. There was nothing whatever they could do.

In the uproar and confusion there was some delay, just enough it seems for the gunman to vanish, for when the police moved into the motel the gunman had gone. However, very close to the motel they retrieved some valuable evidence, a Remington rifle with a telescopic sight, a pair of binoculars and a suitcase, and on the bathroom floor of the rooming house was an empty cartridge case. The murderer had fled, but as it turned out, he had left behind evidence which was to start the massive manhunt we have described. The binoculars were a grisly item of this evidence, for no doubt they had been used by the killer to scan the figures on the opposite balcony until Dr. King was identified without doubt. There was to be no mistake.

Less than an hour after the shooting Martin Luther King, at the age of thirty-nine, was officially declared to be dead in the emergency ward at St. Joseph's Hospital, Memphis.

It is fair to say that all America mourned Dr. King. When the news reached Vine City where his widow, Mrs. Coretta King, lived, the mayor arranged a flight to Memphis for Mrs. King, but, of course, her husband had died before she arrived. The funeral of Dr. Martin Luther King was a great expression of national grief.

It was sheer chance that enabled me to see at first hand the extraordinary early moves in the charges against 'James Earl Ray'. I had been commissioned as a writer to cover the trial of the Kray brothers at Bow Street Magistrate's Court, London. The Krays were said to be the first American-style gangsters in Britain. The two younger brothers, Reginald and Ronald, were accused not only of the murder of an escaped prisoner known as the 'Mad Axeman', they were also accused of being concerned in two fantastic murder attempts, one of them by hypodermic needle concealed in a suitcase which was to spout hydrogen cyanide into the body of the victim. This particular murder plan was to be carried out in the public gallery of the Old Bailey Criminal Court where the victim might consider himself free from murderous attack!

Now it so happened that the case of 'James Earl Ray' came up for hearing in the same court at Bow Street. The Magistrate only was changed. The Chief Metropolitan

Magistrate, Mr. Milton, was sitting in the Kray case, but a Mr. Barraclough, one of his assistant magistrates, sat in the hearing of the extradition proceedings in Ray's case.

The scene was identical. I showed my pass at the door and went straight to the seat reserved for me. The Magistrate sat on a raised bench alone, immediately under the Royal Arms. The court itself, small, smelling faintly of disinfectant, dull brown in its colouring, was as undramatic as it was possible for it to be.

In front of the Bench and seated facing the court room was the Clerk of the Court. Immediately in front of him was the table reserved for counsel who might either be solicitors or barristers pleading in the case that was being heard. Behind the lawyers' table was the dock. To the right of the Bench was the witness box and to the left benches for 'instructing' solicitors.

When I took my seat the court was not yet full. Two or three policemen chatted near the dock, one with walkie-talkie equipment. But soon the scene began to become animated rather in the same way that a quiet night-club will break into life, almost imperceptibly, during the evening.

The lawyers engaged in the case entered and took their seats, undoing the red tape with which their briefs were tied. The Magistrate took his seat. We all stood and again were seated. The prisoner was called and a hatchet-faced man entered guarded by two policemen. There were no handcuffs. One of the policemen indicated the dock to Ray. He entered, bowed to the Bench, and sat down. If this was the start of one of the most sensational criminal procedures of the twentieth century it had a typical London setting. There were to be no histrionics here. The lawyers started to speak. They were audible but only just. The Magistrate sat impassively listening. The press alone showed some excitement as they took down the story in their notebooks.

The habit of many years was not to be broken. Britain has extradition treaties with most countries in the world;

they are, of course, reciprocal. With the United States the treaty provides that American citizens accused of serious crime in their own country might be extradited and brought home for trial and, likewise, British subjects guilty of serious crime in Britain might be extradited from the United States. Extradition is not granted in cases where the nature of the offence is entirely political. It does not as a rule conflict with the granting of asylum to fleeing politicians.

The extradition laws apply to all foreign countries with whom Britain has concluded an extradition treaty. Fugitives within the Commonwealth are covered by the Fugitive Offenders' Act, and extradition is not to be confused with a Government's right to deport foreign nationals. Because American visitors are naturally welcome in Britain, deportation orders (which are a relic of the old Royal Prerogative, now exercised on the Queen's behalf by the Home Secretary) seldom affect Americans, but recently Ralph Shoenman, the author of the idea of a War Crimes Tribunal against the United States, was deported, and, before this, a number of fairly well-known American gamblers were deported because Scotland Yard held the view that what they intended to do in Britain was not 'conducive to public peace and well-being'.

The case of Ramon George Sneyd, as he was known at Bow Street, had attracted public attention because a Mr. Fred Vinson of the American Justice Department had come to London and stated in an airport interview on arrival that his mission was to 'expedite' the extradition of Sneyd. Perhaps the remark was unfortunate. One does not attempt either to expedite or retard legal proceedings in Britain. In fact Mr. Vinson's visit had no effect on the case, which pursued its own proper course.

The applicant for extradition has to show that there is a case against the accused concerning a serious crime. Murder of course is the most serious crime apart from treason. Although the assassination of Martin Luther King had the deepest political motivation and undertones, Sneyd could not possibly say that the charge against him was political in nature.

Sneyd had British lawyers to represent him as well as an American lawyer, Mr. Arthur J. Hanes. Mr. Hanes proved himself adaptable in fastening on to the sedate tempo of the British court. Whether by nature or by design he spoke in the quiet subdued tones adopted by his British colleagues.

I thought, and perhaps most of the trained spectators of these proceedings thought, that the case against Sneyd would be strenuously contested. We expected his lawyers to apply for a writ of 'habeas corpus' to enquire into the reason why Sneyd was being detained and if that reason had validity. But the case took an unexpected turn.

Sneyd did not want habeas corpus proceedings. He said he wanted to return to the United States to establish his innocence.

This of course amounted to the withdrawal of all objections on behalf of the accused to an extradition order. But it did not relieve the Magistrate of the obligation of hearing sufficient evidence to establish that there really was a case against Sneyd that would justify an extradition order being made and the handing of Sneyd over to the American authorities. The evidence was given and the order made.

There followed a remarkable press conference given by Mr. Hanes in which Sneyd's attitude towards the whole matter was fully revealed. This is how the British press reported what was said at this meeting between Sneyd's lawyer and the press:

'Mr. Hanes said Sneyd "has informed the Justice Department and repeated to me on many occasions that he has fear in the presence of Justice agents alone and requested my presence when he is transported to America".

'He could not say what the basis of Sneyd's fear was. "He just does not want to go with them. He has fear and wants me to go with him."

'Mr. Hanes objected to American agents taking Sneyd

to America "in secrecy" and had asked the American Consul in London to tell him when Sneyd is transferred so that he can travel with him.

'He also complained that he had been unable to see his client alone.

'Mr. Hanes and Sneyd's British legal advisers decided late on Tuesday not to apply for a writ of habeas corpus because "we want to get back to America to establish the truth. This is hanging over his head and the sooner it is over the better. He wants to clear his name.

' "It seems to me that Britain wants to get rid of him and the American Government wants to get him, so I think the matter can be dealt with expeditiously. My client is innocent."

'Mr. Hanes knew Sneyd only as R. G. Sneyd. When he saw him yesterday he talked normally and had good sense and judgment.

'The American authorities' refusal to let Mr. Hanes see Sneyd alone, and the visit of Mr. Fred Vinson, representative of the American Justice Department, to "view" Sneyd, violated Sneyd's Constitutional rights and a Supreme Court ruling that suspects must not be questioned without their attorney being present.

'Asked if there was a political conspiracy against Sneyd, Mr. Hanes said, "Perhaps this is it."

'American law officials had been preparing a case against Dr. King's assassin with all the resources of Tennessee and the Government. "Until I get a chance to speak to Sneyd I haven't a chance of preparing a case."

'Were the law officials out to get Sneyd? "Every time the prosecution charged a suspect they wanted to convict him," said Mr. Hanes.

' "They will be yelling for somebody's scalp."

'Mr. Hanes thought charges against Sneyd of possessing a forged passport and a firearm and ammunition without a certificate would be adjourned *sine die* by the Bow Street magistrate. Until then an extradition order could not be signed.

'In a written statement Mr. Hanes said he advised Sneyd to waive further efforts to avoid extradition so that he could be transported to Memphis, Tennessee, "the scene of the alleged crime with which he is charged".

'He thanked the British authorities for meticulously respecting Sneyd's rights and the British press for its objectivity.'

If Sneyd was fortunate in receiving a fair hearing in Britain he was also fortunate in having the services of the discreet and able Mr. Hanes, who had, in effect, established the outlines of his client's defence along the lines that seem to ensure that the trial of James Earl Ray will be one of the *causes célèbres* of the American crime scene in the sixties.

My own impression of Sneyd? I thought that he was a complicated man who smelt of intrigue. Whether or not he in fact is guilty we do not know as yet. Was he perhaps a decoy to take the hunters away from their true quarry? What was his real business as he flitted around Europe, a shabby, somewhat sinister figure escaping from some pursuing doom?

And if Sneyd in fact should be guilty, who told Sneyd to do it? Who paid him? Who provided him with the fairly large sums that enabled him to escape? If this man was a puppet, who pulled the strings?

The British television programme 'Twenty-four Hours' ran a bold commentary on the case in which it was strongly suggested that Sneyd had powerful sponsors who had helped him to escape.

Sneyd was flown out of Britain in a secret operational night exercise. He was handcuffed to two guards and protected by a steel bulletproof waistcoat. The authorities seemed to take the view that there would be interested parties who were determined that Sneyd should not live to say too much. The accused murderer was now a potential murder victim.

The figure of the lone assassin was becoming too familiar on the American political scene. The public was starting to doubt the allegations that these men conceived and executed political assassinations themselves. If in fact they were merely agents of a ruthless murder syndicate, then this would eventually come into the open and the case of Ramon George Sneyd might lead to other prosecutions which could root out the vile plant of violent killing from the American political scene.

20

The Second Strike

THE assassination of Senator Robert Kennedy on Wednesday, June 5, 1968, reverberated around the world. In Britain, by a spontaneous gesture of grief, flags were flown at half-mast. There was not a country in the world that did not believe that a good and potentially a great man had been done to death. Following on the assassination of his brother, four years earlier, millions of men and women in a hundred different countries felt that the kind of dynamic liberalism for which the brothers stood had received a terrible and unexpected blow.

In Britain, perhaps, the horror and the grief were felt more than in any other country except the United States itself. At times like this the rough path of Anglo-American friendship is seen suddenly to become smooth and the grief of one country is the sorrow of the other.

The close ties which the Kennedy family had with Britain accentuated and deepened the distress we felt. When the father, Joseph Kennedy, was American Ambassador in London during the last war, the sons saw the Battle of Britain for themselves. It made them speak of this country in terms of affection and respect ever since.

As recently as January, 1967, Senator Kennedy attended an Anglo-American conference at the Ditchley Foundation near Oxford. He devoted a part of his speech to urging Britain to resume her role of world leadership and concluded with this remarkable exhortation:

'If we are going to find some answers to the problems of the undeveloped world, if we are to find some answers to the problems of Germany, and if we are going to see an historic rapprochement with the Soviet Union, if we are going to find an answer to human beings, including the next generation of Englishmen and Americans, living together on this globe over a period of more than the next 30-40 years, then I think that Great Britain has to play a major role.'

The thread of the English interest which the Kennedys always carried with them and often wove into the pattern of their speeches was discernible again just before the senator met his death. He had won the primary in California. They were waiting for him in the Embassy Room to make his victory speech. In the royal suite his family and closest supporters were gathered, his wife Ethel, his sister Jean and a dozen others. Two or three reporters tackled the senator. One of them said that Gene McCarthy was beginning to act less like an intellectual and more like a politician. Robert Kennedy said: 'I like politicians— and I like politics. It's an honourable adventure.' One of the reporters noted the phrase and Robert Kennedy, seeing this, said: 'You don't remember Lord Tweedsmuir? He was John Buchan, the Scottish author and statesman. He wrote *The Thirty-Nine Steps* and several other good books. Then he was Governor-General of Canada. It was he who said that "politics is an honourable adventure".'

Robert Kennedy stood there thinking aloud and as he did so he repeated the phrase . . . 'an honourable adventure'. It was the last quotation he was ever to make.

The results kept coming in. At first it had seemed that a defeat was likely, even probable. But then the tide turned. The irresistible magic of this man had done its work. It was not going to be a runaway victory, but it was victory. Robert Kennedy was heard to say: 'I am not interested in figures. I am content to win.'

The tension was building up now and the crowd in the hall downstairs was growing impatient. Pierre Salinger had to try to keep the supporters happy while they were waiting. On television he said: 'The senator is coming down here to talk to you in about an hour.'

At half-past eleven the senator's advisers thought that he might go down now and meet his supporters, but Robert Kennedy wanted to be certain. 'Are you quite sure we've won?' he asked.

'Everybody says you've won.'

Apparently Kennedy was not satisfied with this, for it was not until three minutes past midnight that he finally got up and strode towards the door on his way to meet his destiny. Two minutes later he was mortally wounded.

Lurking in the pantry through which Robert Kennedy had to pass was Sirhan Bishara Sirhan, carrying a .22 revolver. He fired eight shots before he was overpowered by Roosevelt Grier, the huge professional football player and the Olympic Champion, Rafer Johnson, among others. In the struggle Sirhan, who fought like a maniac, sprained his ankle and broke one of his fingers. The police had the greatest difficulty in getting him out of the hotel alive. If they had not acted with great speed and toughness, Sirhan would undoubtedly have been lynched. The senator's appalled and angry supporters would have torn him to bits.

Robert Kennedy lay on the floor apparently dying. His wife managed to reach him through an insufferable and suffocating crowd. In her shock and fury she was able to make a little room. The ambulance seemed to be an unconscionable time in coming. When at last it did arrive the senator was almost dead but he had not died. The first medical reports suggested that he might even recover eventually, but whether he would be paralysed or not or whether he would be in command of his full faculties no one knew. In fact it was a hopeless battle. The damage to the brain was far more serious than at first it appeared to be. The team of doctors worked on their patient through the night. Everything that medical science and human ingenuity could do was done, but to no avail. Next day Robert Kennedy died.

Apart from the stunned horror which this atrocious crime provoked, the interest in this last great assassination seems to lie in attempting to answer the question why did Sirhan Bishara Sirhan allegedly commit this awful deed?

I have been writing on Arab affairs for the past ten years and this has made it necessary for me to visit, sometimes for long periods, Jordan, the United Arab Republic, Syria and Lebanon. Knowing as I do the depth of feeling which all Arabs have concerning their long and bitter dispute with Israel, at least I can understand how this alleged crime came about.

It is very difficult for those who have not experienced Arab resentment at first hand to realise that the restoration of what they regard as their homeland to the Arabs is to them a Jihad. It is no longer a matter for argument, for negotiation, or for compromise. It is a matter for which some are willing to die. Sirhan, when he allegedly shot Robert Kennedy, was willing to die.

June 5th was the anniversary of the Arab-Israeli war. Mayor Yorty somewhat indiscreetly gave us the information that when the police searched the Sirhan family house in Pasadena they found two notebooks in which Sirhan had written the words: 'Kennedy must be assassinated before June 5th.'

In the middle of May, Senator Kennedy had made a speech strongly supporting the supply of arms to Israel. It was probably this that finally induced Sirhan to become a dastardly political assassin.

If we look back into the history of Sirhan Sirhan we find that the pieces of the puzzle do seem to fit together into some terrible but not altogether illogical pattern.

Sirhan's father worked for the British under the old mandate of Palestine during a period when Arab and Jew lived together in peace. The family fled during the Arab-Israeli war of 1948 and found themselves a shabby home in the old city of Jerusalem. It was that part of the city which was later to become Jordanian territory.

From the beginning Sirhan was of the material of which fanatics are often made. As the boy grew up he neither smoked nor drank and did not consort with women. Sirhan was undoubtedly influenced in his political philosophy and attitudes by President Nasser who is the hero of young Arabs in whatever country they may be living. Sirhan's political activities were suspect and he was investigated on more than one occasion; it was probably this that proved a factor in the move which the family made to America. Even so there is a deep puzzle here. Every account we have of Sirhan from those who knew him best describe him as diligent, quiet, neat and well-behaved.

Inevitably it will be asked: was Sirhan mad either in the legal sense that his mental balance was so disturbed that he did not realise what he was doing, or in the popular sense that he was so abnormal that the ordinary restraints meant nothing to him? I think it is quite clear that he was neither. This was a deliberate premeditated act. The gun used seems to have been purchased for this very purpose. Sirhan had learnt to use it in order to kill Robert Kennedy and for no other reason. The day on which the murder was committed, June 5th, shows clearly the motive for the crime. It may not be the only motive. It may be that Sirhan was being used by others, but I have no doubt that in his mind he was avenging the terrible and mortifying defeat of the Arab armies by the Israelis in the June war of 1967, exactly one year earlier.

Robert Kennedy was a conspicuously brave man. After the murder of his brother he knew perfectly well that if he pursued politics he was walking with death. When Martin Luther King was murdered in April, a friend said to Robert Kennedy: 'This must bring terrible memories back to you.'

Kennedy thought for a moment and then said: 'Well, yes, it does and it makes me think of what they may do to me, too.'

The death threats which Robert Kennedy received had

grown in number just before he died. They were sorted and sifted by the police and by his aides, and those that appeared to be really menacing were made the subject of investigation. Kennedy was asked to take more care, but how could he do this? The whole complicated election process of the American tradition is based on the candidate meeting the people. It is an old saw of American politics that a hand shaken is a vote won. Moreover Kennedy was of Irish descent. He liked meeting people. To win them over was the kind of challenge he readily accepted. To give up his personal mixing with the multitude would rob him of the most valuable weapon of his campaign. For when the crowd saw the slim figure, the tousled hair, the creased face and that characteristic combination of diffidence, defiance, passion and humour, it evoked in them a particular and spontaneous response. They saw through him back to his brother. These two men had been the knights of the modern American saga. If there was hope of bringing peace to this great country with its diverse races, that hope rested largely in the image which John and Robert Kennedy stood for.

The brothers were, of course, as so many political figures have been in the past, remarkable contradictions. They were rich but they fought for the poor. They were privileged but they championed the underprivileged. They were intellectually brilliant but they appeared to carry the burdens of those who were heavy laden and often uneducated. They were elegant, yet they moved with ease and with obvious pleasure among the great, sweating, vociferous crowds who followed them everywhere. They were essentially and characteristically American, yet in their thinking they were international, which accounts for the fact that the whole world felt that they had a share in the Kennedy vision.

The killing of Robert Kennedy has by now been described many times, but there are still some comments to make on it that I have not seen in public print.

The Ambassador Hotel, which Kennedy had made his

headquarters, does not seem to have been the subject of serious security arrangements. Many people were able to get into the hotel without a pass. This was inevitable without changing the whole pattern of the election. The image which the campaign managers build up so successfully is that of a public hero surrounded by his fervent supporters. How is it possible to keep out the one evil enemy without putting restraint on all those who wish to express their loyalty and devotion?

When Robert Kennedy left his room he stopped for a moment to shake hands with Jesus Perez, who had been washing up dishes and was drying his hands. Kennedy was still shaking the hand of Perez when the gunman fired. Some witnesses say that he was only five feet from his victim. In any case it was a point-blank killing. It was almost a miracle that Robert Kennedy did not have his brains blown out and die on the spot.

This brings us to the curious point that a .22 revolver is not a professional assassination weapon. It is not a killer's gun. It is a gun which only an amateur would use for murder. This contrasts vividly with the complicated and highly lethal weapon used to kill the late President Kennedy. Of course, the elder brother was killed from a distance, possibly by a fusillade of shots, whereas Robert was slain by a man who appeared suddenly with nothing but a serving counter between him and his victim. Witnesses have said that he used the counter to steady his right hand which held the gun. This again does not sound like the behaviour of a man skilled in the use of firearms. The whole dreadful affair has a ghastly amateurish aspect.

When the shots rang out, the crowd of supporters who had been making a cheerful noise in their excitement was stricken by appalled horror. A priest appeared from nowhere and placed a rosary in Robert Kennedy's hand. The hand of Robert Kennedy closed on the rosary. There was a shout for a doctor. Ethel Kennedy fought her way to the figure of her husband who was lying on the floor. Her life had been torn up and her grief could find no words.

The police arrived and took Sirhan into custody, hustling him out of the hotel in one rush, not stopping till they reached their patrol car. Witnesses said that this saved Sirhan's life.

The pandemonium that broke out when the shooting started was understandable. Robert Kennedy was the only man to die at the hands of the assassin, but others had been hit as Sirhan continued to fire wildly. Some of the victims were hit by the same bullet which had ricocheted.

William Weisel of the American Broadcasting Company was wounded in the stomach. A Mrs. Elizabeth Evans had a head wound. Ira Goldstein of the Continental News Service had a hip wound. Paul Schrade, a director of the United Auto Workers, had a serious head wound. There is evidence that the bullets had been treated after the manner of dum-dum bullets to ensure that they would do the utmost damage.

It was thought at this moment in time that Robert Kennedy was likely to die as he lay on the concrete floor. The priest administered extreme unction. It was more than twenty minutes before the ambulances arrived and over half an hour before Robert Kennedy reached hospital. By that time, at Good Samaritan, a team of specialists had been assembled, mainly neuro-surgeons. The doctors fought to save the life of Robert Kennedy. Hope flickered quickly only to die. The magnificent physique of the man kept his heart beating. For him there was no recovery and the only comfort which his family and his friends could take from the agony was the thought that if he had survived he might have been a hopeless cripple without the use of his mental processes. Such a life for Robert Kennedy would have been inconceivable. This man depended on the flame which burnt inside him. If that light was to be put out Robert Kennedy would have had no use for his body.

There has been a searching public post mortem in the United States concerning many aspects of this dreadful crime. Guns have always been part of the American way of life. Hunting is a great national pastime. The tradition of carrying arms or having a gun in the house clearly goes back to frontier days when the gun was a symbol of security and the only real answer to the marauder and the bad man. It is not for a foreign writer to say whether it will be possible to control the sale and use of firearms in the United States. Certainly it would be an immense task. But if the traffic in arms was controlled would it stop political assassination? Cannot the determined assassin always acquire a weapon? It may well be that the assassinations of John and Robert Kennedy and of Martin Luther King were all part of the pattern of turbulence and violence which is shaking the world. This pattern of violence would appear to be fostered by the tension of the times and this in turn can perhaps be accounted for by the fact that in the international field as well as in domestic politics during the last ten years not one major solution has been found.

Racial issues, not only in the United States, are more acute than ever. The Vietnam war has not been brought to a successful conclusion. France recently lurched to the edge of the precipice of anarchy and only drew back at the last moment. Britain has had dangerous economic difficulties. The Communist threat, which never ceases, was defeated in Greece and then only by the intervention of a military dictatorship. The upsurge of the student-anarchist is not a matter to be treated lightly. It is a symptom of the general malaise. And, of course, twenty-two years after the first United Nations resolution aimed at settling the Arab-Israeli dispute, that dispute is more terrifying and more bitter than it was even before the war of June, 1967.

I have no doubt that it was this climate of menace and hopelessness, over which the black shadow of ultimate destruction constantly hovers, that has encouraged these three assassinations which are without parallel in American history.

Is it possible for the American people to alter the pattern of their elections? Is it desirable that they should do so? American elections are largely out-of-door affairs in which the candidate, the centre of attention, meets the maximum number of people. The kind of indoor meeting that is common in Britain at election times would not, I think, be enough for an American public. That public is made up of many nationalities far more extrovert and sometimes excitable than the Anglo-Saxon stock. There is no doubt that the American method of open electioneering on a huge scale secures a rapport between the candidate and his supporters which is not equalled in any other country in the world. So these two questions of gun control and election control will be debated, and some way may be found to secure greater safety for famous figures in the heat of an election campaign.

There is one thing that all Americans and their friends may be glad of—that is, in this truly terrible case, the legal procedure is being scrupulously observed. Moreover security in relation to this prisoner is being made so tight as to be unbreakable. After the police had successfully rescued Sirhan and had him in custody, it was obvious that an attempt might be made on his life in the manner used by Ruby to murder Oswald. The most stringent precautions were taken to prevent this happening, and from the manner in which this case was put before the grand jury, whose duty it is to make certain that there is a case for the prisoner to answer—not a difficult duty in this event—it is clear that Sirhan will be accorded all those protections which the American judicial system guarantees to any and every accused man.

There appears to be no defence. Sirhan's words: 'I did it for my country' explains sufficiently the tortuous, illogical thinking of the man. In fact, of course, he has not helped the Arab cause. He has done it serious, if not irreparable, damage.

So what are we to say as a final word? I suppose that history, removed from the anger and the grief evoked by the killing of this fine man, will say that this was a classical assassination by a fanatic whose deed was the child of his own hatred and of the humiliation of his people.

One last point that I find fascinating and that I have not seen mentioned in all the words I have read on the killing of Robert Kennedy. The Arabic word 'Sirhan' means 'the wanderer'. 'Bishara' means 'good omen'. Sirhan Bishara Sirhan had wandered far from his homeland, but he was an ill omen for the country of his adoption.

Index